WHY THE Cross Can Do
WHAT Politics Can't

When they see you, do they see Jesus?

ERWIN W. LUTZER

D1040490

HARVEST HOUSE PUBLISHERS
Eugene, Oregon 97402

Cover by Koechel Peterson & Associates, Minneapolis, Minnesota

WHY THE CROSS CAN DO WHAT POLITICS CAN'T
Copyright © 1999 by Erwin W. Lutzer
Published by Harvest House Publishers, Eugene, Oregon 97402

Library of Congress Cataloging-in-Publication Data

Lutzer, Erwin W.
    Why the cross can do what politics can't / Erwin W. Lutzer.
        p. cm.
    ISBN 1-56507-998-1
    1. Holy Cross. 2. Christian life. 3. Church and the world.   I. Title.
BT453.L87 1999
227.3'0829—dc21   98-41131
                                                                           CIP

Printed in the United States of America

99 00 01 02 03 /BP/ 10 9 8 7 6 5 4 3 2 1

For Daryle and Jean Worley, our faithful friends and partners in sharing the message of the cross in the heart of Chicago.

"I thank my God every time I remember you" (Philippians 1:3).

Contents

What Kind of Cross
Does the World See?

The prediction was both astonishing and accurate.

In 1834, 100 years before Hitler, a poet named Heinrich Heine assessed the mood in Germany and concluded that only the cross of Christ was holding back the Germans' "lust for war." The prediction was even more remarkable because Heine was a Jew, a man who nevertheless believed that only Christianity could tame what he called that "brutal German joy in battle."

Heine, who possibly did not understand why the cross had supernatural power, called it a talisman, an object with magical power that held aggression at bay in the German nation. And should the cross be broken, he said, the forces of brutality would break out and the world would be filled with "terror and astonishment."[1]

Parallels between Nazi Germany and America can be easily overdrawn, but Heine's assessment might be just as applicable to us as it was to pre-war Germany. Hitler's swastika was a *hakenkreuz* (hooked or broken cross) that replaced the cross of Christ in the German churches. Swastika banners with the cross of Christ in the center were hung in the churches and paraded throughout Germany. When this pagan cross replaced the cross of the crucified Redeemer, the world trembled. This confusion of crosses beguiled the German church and invited the judgment of God.

What if it is true that we could say about America as Heinrich Heine said about Germany—that only the cross of Christ is keeping America from forces of brutality, which, if unleashed, would cause the whole world to be astonished? Do we not already see such forces at work, with the escalation of crime, the moral collapse in our schools, and the destruction of our families?

Today, it is tempting to wrap the cross of Christ in the flag, to equate the American dream with God's dream for this nation. We have attached a myriad of agendas to the cross of Christ, often clouding the one message that the world needs to hear with clarity and power. Ask any average American what Christians believe and he will give you multiple answers, some correct, others misleading. Few will say that the central doctrine of Christianity is that Christ came into the world to save sinners.

Have we (I speak to those of us who are committed Christians) forgotten that God's power is more clearly seen in the message of the cross than in any political or social plan we might devise? Might not our search for some antidotes to our grievous ills be symptomatic of our lost confidence in the power of the gospel to change people from the inside out? Do we cling to the cross with deep conviction that it is not simply *a part* of our message, but correctly understood, the *whole* of it?

Incredibly, the church has, for the most part, abandoned the very message that is most desperately needed at this critical hour of history. At a time when we need to engage our culture with the one truth that has any hope of transforming it, many among us have turned aside to fight the world on its own terms and with its own strategies. The temptation of the church has always been to confuse the kingdom of this world and the kingdom of God, and we are reaping the results.

We are tempted to think that our times are unique. But the fact is that the disciples and their followers had all of our national woes times ten; and yet without any political base, without a voting bloc in the Roman senate, and without as much as one sympathetic Roman emperor, they changed their world, turning it "upside down" as Luke the historian put it (Acts 17:6).

We dare not approach the cross with cool detachment. It exposes the futility of our self-righteousness; it reminds us that we are sinners incapable of bringing about our own reconciliation with God. Before this cross we can stand only with bowed heads and a broken spirit.

And herein comes the warning. P.T. Forsythe, when speaking of the cross as the focal point of God's work for sinners, wrote, "If you move faith from that centre, you have driven *the* nail into the church's coffin. The church, then is doomed to death, and it is only a matter of time when she shall expire."[2] The church can only live and breathe at the cross; without it there is no life and no reason to exist.

This book is based on two fundamental premises. First, *that the problems of America are too far gone to be remedied by a change of administrations in Washington and other levels of government.* Of course Christians should be involved in the political process, particularly in a democracy where the participation of the populace is welcomed and necessary. And, it is important that we elect those whom we believe will make the best decisions for our nation and its families. But we dare not think that solidifying Christians into one voting bloc to confront the world with our own version of political power will actually change the direction of our disintegrating culture.

We face two dangers. One is to say that we should retreat from our social and political battles, and return to the fifties and sixties, when the church was largely uninvolved in politics and culture. Given the political disappointments Christians have had in recent years it would be easy to think that we need to withdraw back to our Sunday schools and Bible conferences, witnessing as best we can, but abandoning the world to its well-deserved fate.

This would be a mistake. The question is not whether we should be involved in our cultural battles; the question is whether we are willing to fight the right battles in the right way. I am not advocating a return to the days when evangelicals existed as a Christian subculture, unknown to the world. The answer is not isolation, but confrontation—with the right attitude and the right message. It would be a tragedy indeed if we just got accustomed to the darkness.

However, the other danger is that we become so overburdened with social/political issues that our message is lost amid these skirmishes. Thus the cross that is exposed to our culture loses its power because its message is clouded with all kinds of agendas that obscure its meaning. The cross that the world sees does not resemble the one found on the pages of the New Testament.

As we shall see, the cross has implications for the whole of life, but we must be careful that we correctly identify the enemy and fight him with the right weapons. We must not let the world define our agenda. Nor can we hope to fight the world with its own methods. Our nation needs an antidote that is far more radical than politics could ever be.

The second premise of this book is my deep conviction that *our so-called culture war is really a spiritual war.* In other words, our problems are not fundamentally abortion, trash television, and homosexual values. The roots of our cultural decay is first and foremost spiritual; we must attack the root of this corrupt tree. As always our greatest challenge is theological, not political or cultural.

Perhaps you have heard the story of the Keeper of the Spring. There was a man who lived high in the mountains who had the responsibility of keeping the spring pure. He removed trash, dead animals, and rerouted contaminated streams in the vicinity of the spring that gushed clear water. But the town beneath the mountain was short on money and, to balance the budget, decided to cancel the man's salary. They argued that people seldom saw him, and the stream would probably remain pure by itself. And it did, for a short while. But within a few weeks the stream was filled with fungus, and an epidemic spread throughout the village.

No doubt some members of the town council advocated measures to clean up the water supply with the latest chemicals. These measures were of some value; the epidemic slowed. At the next mayoral election, candidates vied for theories by which the "water problem" could be solved. The wisest among them suggested that they rehire the Keeper of the Spring, for it was on the top of the mountain that the contamination took place.

This book is a modest attempt to have us return to the top of the mountain, to return to the source of our power and authority.

My clear purpose is to challenge the church to confront the world with the one message that is able to transform society, one life at a time. Yes, we must fight social evils; we must attempt to use whatever means we have to clean up our contaminated culture. But all of our efforts will be futile unless we go to the source of our defilement.

If there is any good news in America, Christians must proclaim it. The truly good news will not come from Washington in the form of new legislation or a proclamation from the president, or even the Supreme Court. The contents of the good news that we must proclaim is the purpose of this book.

Yes, there is a cure for the darkness. We must return to the cross, bowing in submission to the One who was crucified on it. And until we are willing to humbly carry this cross into the world, often at great personal cost, every victory will be fleeting and superficial. We can be involved in legislation and moral crusades, but let us not think that this is the way to transform society.

As I will attempt to show, it is our society's view of God, and not society's view of morals, that lies at the heart of our dilemma. Our nation's love affair with perversity and violence will never end until we as Christians set the agenda and turn this nation to the truly great issues of our time.

Someone has said, "There is no cure for the darkness of midnight except the rising sun. Only when the Son of Righteousness shines forth the darkness must disappear." The cross can shine a light much more powerful than political victories.

This is the time when we take our message to every part of our nation. We must be convinced that we have chosen the wrong path because we have chosen the wrong god. So our first agenda is to return to the message that made the church great.

The Cross and Culture Clash

The cross has always clashed with popular culture.

Come with me to the city of Rome, set majestically along the Tiber River, its citizens stirring to a new day, quite confident that the future would be much like the past. Rome had lasted for 800 years and there was no reason to think that it would not continue for another 800.

On the morning of August 24, A.D. 420, the citizens awoke, startled to discover that traitors were within their gates. During the night, Alaric, the Goth, had overpowered the guards at the Salarian gate, and enemy troops were in the streets. At dawn the looting began.

The barbarians trashed the city, smashing works of art, hoarding treasure, and harassing the citizens. Most disheartening was the participation of the Roman slaves in the looting. The powerless Romans could do little more than watch, feebly protesting the invasion.

When the Goths left three days later, their carts were loaded with gold, silver, and works of art. The city had not been burned, only punished; not destroyed, but humiliated. Some leaders had been killed, but for the most part, Rome could still function—crippled to be sure, but not devastated. Jerome, the great historian, remarked that "Rome had taken the world, but was now taken *by* the world."

Quite naturally the question arose: "Who is to blame?" The citizens sought for a scapegoat, a reason why such a humiliation could have occurred. Their fingers pointed toward the Christians. This was, after all, "their city."

To understand this accusation, we must turn the clock back to about 100 years before this humiliating invasion. In A.D. 312, just before Constantine crossed the Milvian Bridge to conquer Rome, he saw a vision which said, "In this sign conquer," and he interpreted his vision as the sign of the cross. So he marched his soldiers to the river and had them baptized as Christians. The sign of the cross was emblazoned on their shields, and they went forth to conquer in the name of Christ.

Constantine, encouraged by his famous mother, Helena, promoted Christianity, believing that the church might unify the empire, providing a new force that would save classical culture and the empire itself. Indeed, he saw religion as so important that he gave the opening speech at the famous council of Nicea, which was convened to hammer out the doctrine of the deity of Christ. Constantine was not a theologian and cared little for the finer points of Christology. But he told the delegates that doctrinal division was worse than war; he wanted the church to be unified so that the empire could be unified. By the next generation, Rome was Christianized.

How did the pagans accept the Christian takeover? As we might guess, they resented it. In point of fact, many of them continued to hold to their pagan beliefs, refusing to conform to Christianity even outwardly; they clung to their pagan ideas, believing that their own gods were just as helpful as the God of the Christians.

Others only added Christian doctrines to those they already held, bringing their paganism into the church, and the church often accommodated them. They had, for example, believed in many gods; they had a god to invoke when they wanted to sell an object and another god when they wished to buy an object, and another when they took a journey. With the coming of Christianity, they could not continue to be polytheists, but the gods could retain their function if they were thought of as saints to whom the faithful could pray. Now when they took a journey, they prayed to saint Jude, or saint Christopher, and so on. Needless to say, for many people, the conversion to Christianity was external only.

Now that Rome had been humiliated by the Goths, there was a backlash against the imposition of Christian doctrine. The populace rose up to say that their own pagan gods would have done a better job of defending Rome than the Christian God. Indeed, Rome had become great under the dominion of pagan deities. The Christian God stood idly by, watching the barbarians ram the gate, and did nothing. Could a God like that be trusted? This was Rome, the center of Christendom ... if the Christian God was all-powerful, why did He not intervene to defend His city? Why should the Christian gospel be proclaimed if God was indifferent to the plight of those who were called by His name?

Christianity faced a crisis in confidence.

Imagine what would happen in our day if Christians "reclaimed America." Imagine this country with a distinctively Christian president, a committed Christian congress, and a biblically based supreme court. Suppose that at last, Christians were in power and could make the Bible the law of the land. Suppose that we could have compulsory prayer in schools, the criminalization of abortion, and governmental denunciation of homosexuality. Suppose freedom of speech was reinstituted for Christians giving graduation speeches, and that it would be legal to have Christ portrayed in Christmas pageants. America would be as Christian as some modern religious zealots would like her to be.

Then further, let us suppose that soon after this "takeover" there would be an economic collapse that would threaten the very existence of the nation. Suppose there would be wide-spread layoffs, the banks would foreclose, and even the rich would be hard pressed to survive. Imagine soup lines in Los Angeles, New York, and Chicago. All this in our "Christian" nation!

The pagans would be angry! Editorials would call for a return to secularism; talk shows would ridicule the claims of Christians that if only *they* had a chance, America would be great again. Remember, when people are hungry they will always act as if their bodies are more important than their souls. Christians would be blamed for the economic catastrophe, the layoffs, and the soup lines. Many critics would openly say that they would prefer an adulterous president with a strong economy to a Christian president whose policies have led to this fiscal disaster. The credibility of our witness would be challenged.

Just so, the Christians in Rome had to grapple with the fact that Rome was "Christian" and yet destroyed. They had to answer the critics who boasted that pagan deities would have been more vigilant in defending the city. They had to face the fact that their national humiliation happened during their watch.

Two Different Cities

To reply to the critics, Augustine wrote a book titled *The City of God.* He attempted to vindicate "the glorious city of God against those who prefer their own gods to the founder of that city." This "glorious city" was not Rome, but an eternal city that God was building. Augustine defended the God of the Christians, insisting that the sack of Rome did not reflect unfavorably on His character. God had more important purposes than keeping the city of Rome intact. In fact, Rome was wicked, and thus the invasion was justified, even on human terms.

Specifically, there are two cities: the city of God and the city of man. The city of man is built by men and reflects his dreams, hopes, and pride. This city is earthly, temporal, and capable of being destroyed. In fact, it will eventually be totally obliterated.

There is, however, another city, the city of God. This city endures forever; this is the kingdom of God that gives meaning to the world; this is the city of the patriarchs and the prophets, the city of the apostles and the church. This is the city "which hath foundations whose builder and maker is God."

Two different cities means two different citizens. The city of man is populated by those who live by their own laws; they are self-seeking, materialistic, and earthbound. They live their lives according to the rules of fallen human nature. Obviously, to them the destruction of Rome was a great catastrophe.

In contrast, the city of God is comprised of true Christians who follow God's laws and values. These citizens see beyond the earthly to the heavenly. To them, the destruction of Rome was not a travesty. In fact, the pillage of this earthly city could not deprive them of something that had real value because their treasure was in heaven, out of reach of the barbarians.

These citizens set their sights on the unseen spiritual world, which has a higher priority than the temporal. God stands above history as we know it; He is not bound by the course of human events. These are followers of the cross, not the emblems of human government.

These two cities can never be allies, for they represent two different origins, goals, values, and kings. "By two cities I mean two societies of human beings, one of which is predestined to reign with God from all eternity, the other doomed to undergo eternal punishment with the devil."[1] In eternity past only the city of God existed; since the fall of man the two cities have coexisted, but in the future they will be separated, each with its own eternal destiny. Our present responsibility is to live in both cities, giving each its due. We must give to Caesar that which is Caesar's and to God that which is God's.

Augustine did not mean that the city of man is destitute of all civil righteousness and justice. Yes, pagans have built great civilizations, thanks to the virtues they inherited as those created in the image of God. Indeed, Christians should be actively involved in the city of man, building it, maintaining it, and working alongside of those headed to destruction. But Christians should also have no illusions about building an earthly utopia, for they must pass this life with continual opposition from the citizens of the city of man. They must march through the crumbling empires of the world, spreading the knowledge of the gospel.

How, then, shall we live on earth as citizens of heaven?

America: The City of Man

The conflict between the city of man and the city of God rages on in America today. The city of God is trying to find its way amid the growing influence of the city of man. The antagonism between the two cities is sharp and unyielding.

In the next chapter I will give more details regarding the present conflict between the cross and the flag. But here we must simply remind ourselves that the citizens of the city of God are frustrated and angry as they see the daily disintegration wrought by the city of man.

In America, the city of man is built on the cult of self-absorption. We have drifted into radical individualism and the privatization of religion. Because truth is deemed to not exist, what we choose for ourselves becomes the truth for us.

Second, as always, the city of man is built on the desires of human nature... it holds the view of Woody Allen, "the heart wants what it wants." Toleration for every form of deviance has become a national icon.

In sum, the city of man is built upon the lie of Eden, "You shall be like God." Regardless of how that godhood is expressed or applied, it bespeaks a lifestyle that puts man at the center of all things and insists that he is number one. Indeed, everyone, it is believed, has the right to approach God (gods?) in his own way and for his own reasons.

You and I know that religious freedom cannot be endlessly tolerated in a country where the city of man is in ascendancy. Moral disintegration combined with radical individualism is constantly in conflict with biblical virtue. Thus the "wall of separation" between church and state is pressed into service to curtail religious expression at every level. Even now, laws are in place that forbid the condemnation of some sins, such as homosexuality.

Imagine a host of people sailing together on a ship, and some of the travelers insisting that they have a right to drill a hole through the bottom on their side of the vessel. Indeed, they have their "rights" they tell us, guaranteed by the Constitution. Those on the other side of the ship are also respectful of freedom, but shout, "Remember, we are on this ship too! Your "freedom" could mean our collective doom!" Thus there is conflict between the rights of individuals and the rights of the larger community.

It is not easy for us to watch the disintegration of our culture; it is not easy to see religious freedom eroded. With the first amendment turned on its head and interpreted in ways the founding fathers would never have dreamed possible, freedom of speech is being taken away in every area of public life. Schoolteachers are telling children that they cannot write papers on the topic of religion; even the word *God* is systematically stricken from textbooks. Along with this comes expansive rights given to pornographers, abortionists, and homosexual advocates.

What do we do?

Today's church faces the same temptation as Peter when the authorities came to get Christ in Gethsemane. It was not easy for him to see Christ led away; he was overcome by the injustice of it all. He reacted to the arrest squad just like a Roman might and struck the servant of the high priest with a sword and cut off his ear. But Christ responded, *"Put your sword back into its place; for all those who take up the sword shall perish by the sword. Or do you think that I cannot appeal to My Father, and He will at once put at My disposal more than twelve legions of angels?"* (Matthew 26:52,53).

The church always faces the temptation of fighting a legitimate battle in the wrong way. We always are tempted to fight the world with the weapons of the world. We are always tempted to use a sword of steel instead of the sword of the Spirit. And today, that temptation is greater than ever.

The Church: The City of God

Thankfully, the Bible has an answer for us. Our present situation is not very different from that of the first-century church. Virtually every letter in the New Testament was written to a church that was an island of righteousness in a sea of pagan values.

For example, Paul wrote the book of Philippians from a jail cell in Rome. It is a letter of optimism written from a city filled with hostility and violence. Who was ruling in Rome? Nero.

There was not a single Christian on the Roman senate. There was no Christian political lobby, no watchdog committee to make sure that the interests of the Christians were being addressed. There were no courts where the false accusations could be justly resolved. Paul sat in a prison in Rome without due representation. The Christians were often falsely accused without having anyone available to set the record straight.

Most of the epistles in the New Testament were written to help the citizens of the city of God to know how to live in the powerful, evil city of man. To readers who faced the hostility of their culture, Paul wrote, "Our citizenship is in heaven" (Philippians 3:20). The Greek word is *politeuma,* from which we get our word *politics.* He says that our citizenship, our *politics,* if you please, "is in heaven."

Paul sketched the difference between the heavenly and earthly citizenship. He was both a citizen of Rome and a citizen of heaven. He recognized that these two cities had two different values, two different loves, and two different lifestyles. It was because Augustine understood Paul that he would write that these two cities "have been formed by two loves: the earthly love of self, even to the contempt of God; the heavenly by the love of God, even to the contempt of self."[2]

Paul spoke movingly of those who thought of themselves as friends of the cross, but in reality they were its enemies:

> For many walk, of whom I often told you, and now tell you even weeping, that they are enemies of the cross of Christ, whose end is destruction, whose god is their appetite, and whose glory is in their shame, who set their mind on earthly things. For our citizenship is in heaven, from which also we eagerly wait for a Savior, the Lord Jesus Christ; who will

transform the body of our humble state into conformity with the body of His glory, by the exertion of the power that He has even to subject all things to Himself (Philippians 3:18-21).

Notice the contrasts between the two citizens:

1. *We walk in different directions.*

"For many walk, of whom I often told you, and now tell you even weeping, that they are enemies of the cross of Christ" (verse 18). We walk where our affections take us, and the cross is despised by the city of man. To them the cross is foolishness. Perhaps Paul is not referring here to the ungodly pagans, but to the Judaizers who claimed to embrace the cross but added to its message. They too are enemies of the cross, and their behavior made Paul weep. You do not have to be a pagan to be an enemy of the cross: you simply have to add human merit as a requirement for salvation. That also renders the power of the cross of no effect.

There are more enemies of the cross than those who say they are; some "friends" of the cross deny its message. They belong to the city of man, even though they profess to belong to the city of God.

More on that later.

2. *We have different desires.*

"... whose end is destruction, whose god is their appetite and whose glory is their shame" (verse 19). Again, in context, Paul might be referring to the Judaizers who believed that what they ate (or did not eat) determined their relationship with God. The phrase "their shame" might refer to the rite of circumcision, which was believed to be the mark of a true Jew. The Judaizers gloried in the shame that accompanied this ritual.

Again, this passage has a wider application. For many people, their god is their appetite, either by taking pride in their diet, or by choosing to overeat and fulfilling every craving of the flesh. Add to this other appetites: alcoholism, drugs, sensuality of every kind. They glory in that which should give them shame.

Think of today's talk shows! The assumption is that if one reveals the most intimate details of his or her sex life on national television that the process will bring cleansing and emotional wholeness. Contemporary man is convinced he can heal his own soul if only he will be open, "honest," and otherwise clever. Thus the most shameful things are revealed, without a twinge of shame. Pity these people as they try to purify their own souls by the dirty water from within! Light is proclaimed as darkness; darkness is proclaimed as light.

The citizens of the city of man are characterized by the pleasurable values of this world. They are deceived into believing that earth can keep its promises, or at least that it is the only life that really matters. One way or another, they do all they can to eke out some happiness as they walk life's road.

Citizens of the city of God have meat to eat of which others know nothing. They know that one shall not live by bread alone, but by every word that proceeds out of the mouth of God. They are learning to be content with God. And they agree with the Puritans who said, "He who has God and everything else does not have more than He who has God alone."

3. *We speak different languages.*

When describing the inhabitants of the city of man, Paul writes that they "set their minds on earthly things?" (Philippians 3:19). Just listen to the talk on a bus or at a barbershop; just listen to what is said in the hallways and corporate boardrooms of our business enterprises. The topics of conversation, and even the jokes, seldom arise above the things of this earth.

"You brood of vipers, how can you, being evil, speak what is good? For the mouth speaks out of that which fills the heart. The good man out of his good treasure brings forth what is good; the evil man out of his evil treasure brings forth what is evil" (Matthew 12:34,35).

In contrast, the citizens of the city of God speak a different language. As pilgrims our speech betrays us. We speak with the recognizable accent of heaven. We are disappointed when our treasures on earth are stolen, but we are not dismayed. We know the difference between the temporary and the permanent; between the seen and the unseen. We rejoice in that which cannot be taken from us.

4. *We have different aspirations.*

The citizens of earth pin all of their hopes on the news that comes to them from earth. They long for the assurance of more wealth, power, and personal aggrandizement. They believe that "you only go around once," therefore they must "grab for the gusto." Their eyes are glued to the latest fluctuations in the stock market, the world of fashion, or the lives and activities of the rich and famous.

Citizens of heaven, however, look for the heavenly king. They "eagerly wait for a Savior the Lord Jesus Christ; who will transform the body of our humble state into conformity with the body of His glory." They look for Him because they love Him and are eager to "see Him just as He is" (see 1 John 3:2).

5. *We will arrive at different destinations.*

Of those who belong to the city of man, Paul says, "[their] end is destruction." They were alienated from God in this life, and will be so in the life to come.

In contrast, we who are citizens of the city of God await the return of Christ and the transformation of "the body of our humble state into conformity with the body of His glory, by the exertion of the power that He has even to subject all things to Himself" (Philippians 3:21). Thus, as Augustine said, the two cities will eventually separate and never meet again.

Dual Citizenship

Clearly, conversion to the city of God necessitates an entire change of worldviews. The citizens of God judge the immediate by the permanent. They see beyond the pleasure, greed, and pride of the city of man. The new birth introduces them into a whole new family, new values, and new lifestyle … and above all, a new future.

But we live in both cities, just as the Christians in ancient Rome. Augustine argued that we must never forget that our purpose lies beyond this life. The meaning of history is not found in the flux of outward events, but in the drama of redemption.

How can we discharge both obligations?

First, we can *withdraw*. That was what the Mennonites and Anabaptists did during the Reformation era. They would have nothing to do with law enforcement, war, or politics. They preserved themselves by having as little contact with the world as possible. The arts, the development of culture, and society in general was evil and to be avoided. Thus they studied the Bible with those who agreed with them, and for the most part abandoned the world to the devil.

This, to a lesser degree, was also the response of the church in America after the Scopes trial (you may remember that was the famous "monkey trial" in which the question was asked about whether evolution should be taught in public schools). Given the vacuum created by the retreat of Christians, Christian ideas in art, history, and culture were replaced by secularism, the cheapness of human life, and a variety of perverse values. Some believers today advocate a withdrawal from politics, saying that no Christian can serve in the city of man without compromise and eventual absorption within the secular culture. Ditto for law, education, and the arts.

I disagree.

Second, there are those who tell us that we should capture the city of man through political power. We should overtake its institutions, its power base, and its courts. Then the city of God can rule over the city of man. To quote Pat Robertson, "The time is not far distant when we're all going to have to gird ourselves and take that long march up to Armageddon to do battle for the Lord."

If ever there was a cultural takeover, it was when the Roman Empire was "Christianized." When the Christians were in power, they used their standing to enforce Christian values and Christian theology. Eventually, the Pope became the highest authority in the land. Indeed, Augustine himself taught that the Lord had given the church two swords: the sword of the Word and a sword of steel. It was the responsibility of the state to enforce God's laws on earth.

The Christians were glad that the tables had been turned. Indeed, during those dark days when the church experienced persecution from the pagan Roman Empire, Christians thought how wonderful it would be if they were in power. Then they would capture the state's institutions and enforce biblical values in every part of the empire.

With the coming of Constantine, their wish was fulfilled. But with the church married to political power, corruption soon ran rampant. And when the church obscured the teaching of the Bible with its traditions, "heretics" were burned at the stake. Woe to the person who did not bow to the authority of the church, for it held "the keys of death and of hell." The hierarchy of the church was convinced that God's will was being done on earth. Incredibly, with the church now "in power" genuine believers were now persecuted not by secular Rome, but by religious Rome. The true believing church insisted that nothing had changed; a sword wielded by a corrupt church hurt just as much as the sword of a pagan.

Today, some leaders tell us that we should "take dominion" of the earth by capturing its power structures and enforcing God's laws. They believe that political power can rescue us from the moral and spiritual oblivion to which we appear to be moving. But is it our responsibility to capture the city of man, overtake it, and make it into a "city of God"? Can we expect the citizens of the city of man to abide by the laws of the citizens of the city of God? More on that later.

The third view, which will be presented in this book, is that we must learn to serve both the city of man and the city of God, with devotion to Christ. We must learn to be salt and light with such spiritual power that society will be changed from the inside out. This approach, as we shall see, asserts that we be involved at all levels of society, but with a distinctly biblical agenda. It is with the recognition that theology is the first mission of the church; this is the way of the cross. It is the way of humility, the way of repentance, and when necessary, the way of suffering.

We all grieve because our society does not reflect Christian values. And we would all agree that in previous generations our society as a whole did have what Francis Schaeffer called "a Judeo-Christian consensus." But there was never a time when this nation was specifically Christian, though there was a time when it was more directly influenced by the Christian worldview.

For example, 100 years ago we did not have a million preborn infants killed in abortion clinics each year; we did not have trash television and homosexuality taught in schools. But back then,

African Americans were not seen as presidential candidates either; racism was deeply felt and taught even in our churches. The rights of minorities were ignored and the poor treated with benign neglect. The "good old days" were not as good as many people remember them to be. In every generation it has always been necessary for the church to return to the core of its message.

Jesus warned that in the last days there would be wars, betrayals, apostasy, iniquity, and violence. And Paul expanded upon this with his own list of sins (2 Timothy 3:1-3). The simple fact is that we will never see all of society transformed; the consequences of our fallen humanity will always be with us. The church will always be a minority in our culture—a powerful minority to be sure, but a minority nevertheless.

Why are we so uptight about the media declaring war on our Christian values? What do we expect from the city of man? Are we hoping for accolades? Why should we think that the cross should be attractive to the world when the Bible pointedly says that it contains a message that will be greeted with hostility? What about Christ's words? *"If the world hates you, you know that it has hated me before it hated you"* (John 15:18).

Why should we expect Hollywood to reflect Christian values when our culture as a whole does not? The movie producers will create any movie that the unconverted masses will pay for. That is how the city of man does business. Now that our Judeo-Christian heritage has been pushed aside, we can expect that homosexuality will be taught in schools and pornography will flourish.

So what do we do?

We must return to those truths that made the church great. We must proclaim a message that is nothing less than the direct intervention of God in our world. Yes, we must fight, but we must fight like Christ, who never wavered from His message of spiritual redemption in the midst of depressing political and social abuses. We have a message that can do what politics can't.

Our Task Today

Back in the sixteenth century, God raised up Martin Luther to combat the political and doctrinal corruption that had accumulated throughout the centuries. Despite Luther's many faults, he recovered the only message that could possibly transform the human heart. He knew that there could not be moral recovery without theological recovery.

First, the Reformation insisted that the Bible alone is a reliable message from God. This means that all other religions—all other prophets, gurus, and revelations—must be rejected. This is a message that must be heard again in our day of pluralism, pop religion, and "words from God" that supposedly come to some of God's prophets.

Of course we must be tolerant of other beliefs, if by that we mean that we must respect the views of others no matter how different they are from our own. But we must combat a mindless tolerance that believes that every opinion is of equal value because it arises from an individual's own experience. Our task is to show the basis for the entire Christian worldview.

Second, the Reformation insisted that salvation cannot be the work of man, but must be the work of God alone. Our responsibility is to share this truth with all clarity and conviction with total dependence upon the Holy Spirit. We must trust God to do the work that no man can do.

Surely we should weep over the statistics that are so often touted by the pollsters: Although a large percentage of people claim to be "born again," only comparatively few can recite the ten commandments or know who preached the Sermon on the Mount. The fact is that many evangelicals proclaim a gospel that is incapable of saving anyone. Thus so often there is no transformation of life, no change of moral and spiritual direction.

Finally, we must understand that only the cross is able to reconcile men and women to God. To "believe in Christ" without a clear picture of our desperate need of Him … and to not understand why His death for sinners was necessary if we are to be saved … will cause our gospel preaching to fall short of "the power of God for salvation" (Romans 1:16).

Indeed, it is possible that you, the reader, have never been "born again" by the power of God's Spirit. If not, or if you lack assurance, let me remind you that apart from Christ we are spiritually dead, unable to contribute to our redemption (Ephesians 2:1-4). But thankfully, God is able to raise the dead and give sight to our blind eyes. In ourselves we do not even have the faith by which we can receive God's forgiveness and redemption.

If we acknowledge this helplessness, God will grant us the ability to transfer our trust to Christ alone, and we will be converted by God. The promise is there: "As many as received Him, to them He gave the right to become children of God, even to those who believe in His name, who were born not of blood, nor of the will of the flesh, nor of the will of man, but of God" (John 1:12,13). Clearly we are saved by God's will, not our own. And again, "In the exercise of His will He brought us forth by the word of truth, so that we might be, as it were, the first fruits among His creatures" (James 1:18).

This is the message of life that is needed in this confused generation. The citizens of heaven must return to doing what only the citizens of heaven can do. We must keep pointing beyond this life to the next, and encourage others to join us on our pilgrimage to the eternal city of God.

Let us say with Thomas Moore, "I die the king's good servant, but God's first."

Two

The Cross and the Flag

Are the American dream and the Christian dream one and the same? If not, how are they different? If America maintains her strength and power, can we be sure that the church will be strong and powerful?

If America's strength crumbles, does it follow that the church will become smaller and weaker? Or is it possible for the church to remain strong even with an economic meltdown and the collapse of political structures?

Is support for tax breaks for families, term limits for congressmen, and backing for the National Rifle Association part of the Christian agenda? What about a strong national defense? Or legislation that would give Christianity a privileged status? Should we fight to put prayer back in our public schools?

The terrain of this chapter is fraught with mine fields! Thanks to our nationalistic instincts it is difficult for us to look at our nation objectively. It is hard for us to face the fact that we as a church might be veering off track, losing sight of our most important goal. It is difficult to admit that we just might have mistaken the American dream for God's dream.

Come with me on a tour of history and Scripture as we search for firm ground upon which we can unravel the entanglements between church and state; God and country; the cross and the flag.

The Christian's Obligation

In order to entrap Him, Christ's enemies posed a question: "Teacher, we know that You speak and teach correctly, and You are not partial to any, but teach the way of God in truth. Is it lawful for us to pay taxes to Caesar, or not?" (Luke 20:21,22).

Remember that the Romans occupied the land, exacting exorbitant taxes, and gloating in their greed. The Jews had no alternative but to pay what was demanded. Needless to say the Romans and their taxes were despised.

If Christ had said "Yes, pay these taxes," He would have been on the wrong side of popular opinion. You could not find a Jew who said that it was good and right to pay taxes to these foreigners, these idolaters. They paid taxes only because they *had* to.

If Christ had said "No, do not pay taxes to Caesar," He could have been turned over to the Roman authorities. To speak openly against Rome was a crime that would not go unpunished.

Christ countered His enemies' question with a request: "Show Me a denarius. Whose likeness and inscription does it have?" (Luke 20:24).

"Caesar's," replied the questioners.

The Jews hated the sight of a Roman denarius—not only because it reminded them of their slavery, but because the image on the coin was idolatrous. In the minds of the pagans, Caesar was a god. Thus, by using the coins, the Jews felt they were being forced to support a state-sponsored idolatrous worship.

"Then render to Caesar the things that are Caesar's, and to God the things that are God's" Christ replied (verse 25).

In other words, *yes*, they should pay taxes to Caesar. Even though Caesar would use the money to pay Roman soldiers to maintain a stranglehold on the Jewish nation, *taxes were to be paid*. The Jewish people were to be subject to the powers that be, however unjust. But—and this is important—the people were also to *pay to God the allegiance they owed Him*.

No one had ever said this before. Christ taught we have an obligation to pay our dues to a corrupt, pagan political regime *and* God. As believers it is possible for us to discharge our obligations to the city of God as well as to the city of man. The spheres overlap and yet are separate.

Years later Christians in the Roman Empire—bless them—argued that they could still be good citizens of Rome even though they worshiped the one true and living God. But Caesar disagreed. To be a good Roman, the authorities insisted, you had to accept the Roman religion. And for those who were not willing to affirm that "Caesar was Lord," the lions were waiting.

Of course when the tables were turned and Rome was "Christianized" there was still no freedom of religion within the empire. As we have already learned, "heretics" were burned at the stake, killed with the sword, or drowned. Often the first victims were genuine Christians who refused to synthesize their faith with prevailing pagan ideas. Small groups who rejected the inherent validity of the sacraments and as a matter of conscience believed in adult baptism were routinely persecuted.

For example, in the year A.D. 400 the Donatists separated from the church, insisting on adult baptism and the belief that a priest had to live a moral life in order for the sacraments to convey grace to the worshipers. These congregations were hunted down, persecuted, and killed—wiped off the face of the earth. The "true" Christians were in charge, and they were determined to run things according to their laws.

As the church became powerful, political appointments were sold to the highest bidder and indulgences were used to fill the church coffers. The doctrinal deviations were so twisted and the political deals so corrupt that Martin Luther and others chose to break from church and, as best they could, return to the faith of the New Testament.

With the coming of the Reformation, conversion was now individualized; personal faith in Christ was proclaimed as necessary for salvation. Neither one's parents nor a priest could make an infant (or an adult for that matter) a Christian. The Reformers knew that no one could be forced to believe—for unless God changes the heart of the individual, there can be no lasting transformation.

When Luther declared, "My conscience is taken captive by the Word of God ... I cannot and I will not recant," he was enunciating a principle that would later lead to freedom of religion: no one can coerce another to believe, thus individual consciences must be respected. Freedom of religion did not immediately follow the Reformation, but it was on its way.

Freedom in America

When the pilgrims came to America, it was to establish freedom of religion, but evidently that wasn't the case for everyone. Roger Williams was banished from New England because he was a Baptist. The Puritans followed the covenant theology of Calvin. They came seeking freedom for the Protestant faith. They would have been scandalized by the idea of religious freedom as we think of it today.

That said, the Puritans (called such because of their emphasis on purity of doctrine) were not sour, gloomy, and world-denying. They agreed with Luther that a person who made good shoes and sold them at a fair price was serving God as much as the clergy. They also believed in a good education not merely in theology but also in the humanities. Doctrinally, they believed in the inability of man to come to God on his own; apart from God's direct, specific intervention an individual cannot be saved. This doctrine made them helplessly dependent on God for the proclamation of the gospel.

However, by the time the Bill of Rights was adopted in 1791, the participants believed that doctrinal agreement was not necessary for the preservation of the union. Of special interest to us is the first amendment with its famous phrase, "Congress shall make no law regarding the establishment of religion nor prohibiting the free exercise thereof."

The intention of this phrase was to limit the power of government—to make sure that the United States did not establish a state church to which all must adhere. Also, the government was not to interfere with religious expression. And most assuredly, it was believed that religion could and should be practiced in the political sphere. Just witness the verses of Scripture engraved in government buildings in Washington, D.C.

The notion that there is a "wall of separation" that allows a rock concert but forbids the singing of hymns in the same park is a construct that modern liberals have used to try to silence the voice of Christians. The idea that a child drawing a picture of the nativity scene on a school chalkboard constitutes government sanction of religion is, of course, absurd. But a secular state will always be hostile to religion and seek to limit its influence.

Where did the idea of religious freedom come from? Most of our textbooks trace it back to the eighteenth-century enlightenment, when advances in science and communication changed the western world. However, as we have already noted, the seeds of freedom were planted in the Protestant Reformation with its emphasis on individual conversion and the freedom of conscience.

Was America a Christian nation? No nation is Christian; the number of true believers is always a minority in any country, America included. Nations do have, however, varying degrees of Christian influence. America was founded as a religious nation, but not necessarily a Christian one. The debates that took place between the early leaders of our country were replete with references to God, but not to Christ. The fact that only about 10 percent of the population attended church during the time of the American revolution is proof enough that America has never been distinctively Christian.

Some of our founding fathers were committed Christians, but they were a minority. Most believed in God but would not have affirmed the deity of Christ, His atoning death on the cross, and His resurrection and ascension. Even when they prayed, it was not to the God and Father of our Lord Jesus Christ, but to a Deistic God who was comfortable with a broad spectrum of religious convictions.

We have only to recall Benjamin Franklin's attempts to undermine Puritan influence and beliefs in Philadelphia, and Thomas Jefferson, who succeeded in removing all courses on the Christian faith from the curriculum at the University of Virginia. He also created his own New Testament, cutting from it every one of the miracles. These examples suffice to remind us that not all the founding fathers were distinctively Christian. Religious yes; Christian, no.

Is it possible to believe in any religion you might choose (or no religion, for that matter) and still be a good American citizen? Can you honor the flag even if you don't believe in God? The founding fathers answered this question by saying *yes* and *no*. Yes, an atheist can still be a bona fide American citizen. But at the same time they believed that the populace could not maintain such magnificent freedoms without the underpinnings of religion. Freedom, they believed, would be so abused by the irreligious that the nation would eventually rot. Without widespread belief in transcendent values, freedom would turn into anarchy, and morality into personal self-interest. Thus America was profoundly influenced by Judeo-Christian values.

The Christian influence in America is eroding daily. Opinion polls show that most Americans believe in God, but many live as practical atheists, paying little attention to the Bible as God's revelation. The proliferation of New Age thought, the radical individualism that clamors for personal rights, and the privatization of morality tears at the very fabric of our families and institutions. Humanism is now coming to its logical conclusions in education, law, and morality. The result is as bad as the founding fathers imagined it might be.

What shall we do?

Should we try to turn the clock back to the supposed "good old days," when we had a shared morality, a widespread respect for

God, and the belief that truth did actually exist? We long for a nation without drugs, abortion on demand, and occultism in our newsstands and television programs. We long for a return to the days when people were embarrassed about adultery and when movies adhered to a minimal standard of decency.

Our first inclination may be to lash out, insisting that it is time to "take this country back." But unfortunately such a mentality betrays the fact that we just might not understand how we got here in the first place. Besides, when we are angry, it is possible to do the wrong thing. As we saw in the previous chapter, we are not in a cultural war but a spiritual conflict. Thus we must fight in God's way and with God's weapons.

The Bible has the answer for us. This is not the first time that the church has had the responsibility of representing Christ when society as a whole has abandoned God. We must recapture the church as an institution for renewal rather than simply an agent for bitter confrontation.

More specifically, we must understand the proper relationship between the cross and the flag, between God and Caesar. We must be able to distinguish the Christian dream from the American dream.

The Cross and the Flag

Certainly God has blessed America because of its Christian influence. But it is misleading to say that America was chosen to replace Israel, and that it was a distinctly Christian nation. We do harm to the body of Christ when we cannot clearly distinguish between the cross and the flag. If we confuse the two, it will be to the detriment and weakness of the church.

Here are three ways to understand the relationship between these two symbols.

The Cross Joined to the Flag

"My country, right or wrong!"

Christians have always been in danger of rendering to Caesar that which is God's. We can subtly become nationalistic, affirming that because our country is great it must also be right and good. It is always easier to see the weaknesses of another country than it is to see the weaknesses of our own. For us, it is hard to determine where the flag ends and the cross begins.

Today some Christian leaders have formed coalitions to "take America back." They want to "put God back" into our political, legal, and educational institutions. With enough numbers and voting power, they think that the hands of the clock can be reversed. They long for a return to a basic civil religion where everyone marches in line with minimal religious convictions.

What is civil religion? Henry Steele, one of America's leading historians, has argued that "the new nation began with two religions, one secular and one spiritual. Almost all Americans acknowledged themselves as Christians," but in fact, "they generally shared what has been called a civil religion...a secular faith in America herself, in democracy, equality, and freedom, which were equated with America in the American mission and the American destiny."[1] "The substance of such a civil religion," writes Michael Horton, is its "tendency to push God to the outer fringes so that He can be called on for state functions, but not get involved in the day to day thinking or operation of normal life."[2]

Ralph Reed, a past president of the Christian Coalition, acknowledged that it was his intention to restore "time-honored civil religion—not to establish Christianity by law or create an official church." We can be glad that it was not his intention to "establish Christianity by law," but as Tom Sine points out, surely he should realize that "time-honored civil religion and

Christianity are two very different faiths." Indeed, Sine writes, these two "bow the knee to two very different deities and work for two very different agendas. Civil religion supports the nationalistic agenda of 'advancing the United States' while Christian faith is committed to advancing God's transnational kingdom."[3] It is incomprehensible how Christians can worship at two different altars and serve two different Gods. But can't we serve both? Yes, but only if we keep them distinct and see where one ends and the other begins.

In a museum in Berlin I saw pictures of the swastika with the cross of Christ in the center. As I gazed upon those pictures, I decided to study the history of the church under Hitler to try to find out why the church had embraced his agenda. The stage had already been set in World War I when young men dying on the battlefield were depicted as martyrs for Christ. These soldiers and many others were convinced that a strong Germany meant a strong church. In my book *Hitler's Cross* I explain how this confusion of crosses led to widespread support of Hitler when he arrived on the scene. The churches at the time were oblivious to the fact that they had traded their biblical faith for the civil religion of Germany, a form of Christianity that called for a powerful defense, a strong economy, and unquestioned patriotism. They were seduced by a subtle confusion of kingdoms.

In more recent years we have seen that promoting civil religion can lead to at least three errors. First, there is the tendency to lump all kinds of issues together and call them all "Christian." Thus abortion, which is a biblical issue, is linked to a balanced budget amendment, lower taxes, and a strong national defense. In our country, all of these issues are often found linked together under the Christian banner.

Only this confusion of values could account for Jerry Falwell, the leader of the Moral Majority, back in the eighties when he made a visit to South Africa and returned supporting the white apartheid government. I've not forgotten this because of a discussion I had with a cab driver in Toronto when Falwell's trip was in the news. When I talked to my driver about his need to accept Christ, he told me that he could not accept Christianity because it supported racism. I tried as best I could to distance myself from the stance Jerry Falwell had taken, but my angry, persistent driver would not allow me the privilege. When we arrived at the hotel he was still castigating Falwell, asking me over and over again how I could be a Christian if one of American's most famous ministers held to a racist point of view.

Of course the Moral Majority no longer exists and no doubt Falwell has had second thoughts about some of the things done and said in earlier times. But the point is that when churches become directly involved in political issues, they obscure the message of the cross. How easily we can create unnecessary stumbling blocks rather than dismantling them. Even as I write, there are various groups with plans to force the hand of some of our politicians to make sure that they follow the "Christian" position on a host of issues.

Second, many of us want a civil religion because we fear that we might lose our creature comforts if our nation goes into decline. We can be glad that Americans have supported mission agencies around the world, but I fear that one reason we are so anxious that the economy remain strong is not because we want to continue to spread the gospel, but because we all enjoy the American way of life. Our tendency is to believe that a strong America always translates into a strong church.

Many Christians today are concerned about corruption in government, the wasting of our taxes, the national debt, and funding of certain types of art projects. However, we are angry not because Christ is daily dishonored and the true God not worshiped, but because we fear that our taxes and family values are not being protected.

To put it clearly: for some Christians, lower taxes, a strong national defense, a rollback of government regulations, and a balanced budget amendment are more pressing issues than whether their neighbors and friends will spend eternity with God or be lost forever. Our creature comforts are the issues that really stir our ire.

I'm convinced that many Christians who are angry today would become pacified if somehow we could return this country to the fifties, when drugs were not rampant, pornography was not available other than on the black market, and movies—for the most part—portrayed family values. They would be satisfied with this change even if no one were converted to Christ in the process! They would be content if Christ were accepted as lawgiver to restore order to society ... even if He were not accepted as Savior to *rescue* society.

While many of us Christians don't like to see artists create pornographic art, we don't get upset because we have come to believe that freedom of expression is the American way. What really makes us angry is not the pornography itself, but the fact that our tax dollars are used to fund it! Now there is an issue that will rally the troops: our pocketbook!

In other words, it is not because people are going to hell that we are upset. It is not the fact that such artists and those who endorse them are on a collision course with God that grieves us. Rather, it is that our way of life is being disturbed. On Christmas day, says Tom Sine, we want our living rooms to look as if there was an explosion in a department store! Isn't that the American way?

Yes, extravagance is the American way. But is it the distinctively *Christian* way? Several years ago, just before Christmas, I visited the country of Belarus, which had just gained independence from communist control. I asked my friend Victor Krutko what the stores carried for the holidays. He looked at me with a wry smile and said, "There is no Christmas shopping; the Christians just sing hymns. There are no presents—the stores are empty and the people have no money." Does that mean they are less Christian than the rest of us? I think not.

The third danger of civil religion is that we are tempted to put our hope in politics. Think of the optimism of those who believed that the election of a conservative Congress in 1994 would reverse Washington's slide into unrestrained liberalism. Two years later the entire mood of the country was reversed and the old players were reelected. And, as I write, Washington seems to be "back to normal"!

A Christian man who worked for Jimmy Carter was painfully disillusioned by the men the president brought to Washington. I say this not to suggest that we should not be involved in politics as Christians (we have both the privilege and obligation to do so), but rather to remind us that we cannot pin our hopes on a political star, not even a "born again" one. If we were honest we would admit that the Republican party has benefited far more from the support of Christian coalitions than Christians have gained from the Republican party. Indeed, some activists are admitting that the "religious right" has come away empty-handed after years of political promises that never were honored. Chesterton was right: A coziness between church and state is good for the state but bad for the church.

Edward Dobson, a former board member of the Moral Majority, changed his mind about the power of politics. He wrote, "Politics cannot offer permanent solutions because it is based on a flawed view of sin and society. One of its premises is that if you elect the 'right' representatives who will pass the right legislation you will have the 'right' society. But we know this is not true."[4] We have forgotten that the reason the world will never share our values is because it does not share our Christ.

Unfortunately, some people think that if we cannot dominate one political party, we must create another party that will finally do the job! We must form a "Christian party" with all the right players who have all of the right convictions. Be assured that such an approach will backfire and fail, even if for a time it appears to succeed.

Many of us know that fundamentalists/evangelicals have always been critical of the theological liberals who ceased preaching the gospel in favor of political and social action. Incredibly, the same charge can now be laid at the feet of the evangelical community, with its emphasis on political muscle, watchdog organizations, and boycotts. The concerns are different, but the methods are the same.

The cross must always stand alone, unopposed by competing loyalties. Its message must never be sacrificed on the altar of our own political or social agenda, or affected by which political party is in office. Of course political policies have an effect on our lives, but right laws cannot make people good, nor can they make godly families. Our message must be more radical than any governmental policy could possibly be. It is a message that must penetrate the depths of the human heart.

The Cross and the Flag

How then do we discharge the dual obligations to which Christ referred? How do we pay our dues to the city of God and the city of man?

In relation to the city of man, we are to pray for those who have the rule over us. We are to pay taxes and we are, as much as possible, to support government policy. As for our duty to God, we must love Him with all our heart, soul, mind, and strength (Mark 12:30). We must return to the gospel of our forefathers, the gospel that came from the supernatural God of the apostles and their followers. Our responsibility in the world is to showcase Christ—to put Him on display so that the world can see what He is able to do in the lives of those who trust Him. We are to show His "worthiness" and invite others to believe in Him.

Our responsibility is not to show the world that we can win at playing its own political game. It is not to prove to the world that we can shout just as loudly when our rights are violated. It is not our responsibility to warn people that they had better follow our morality because we will soon be "taking our country back."

We have a message that must be heard above the din of political posturing and rancor. We have an agenda that is even more important than saving America: it is holding the cross high so that God might be pleased to save Americans.

How must we represent Christ?

Choosing the Right Battle

First, we must *choose the right battle*. Is our real conflict cultural, moral, or political? No, it is doctrinal and spiritual. We can argue that Christian morality is better; we can try to clean up our culture by legislation and boycotts. But our efforts will be like trying to mop up the floor with the faucet running. We are trying to convince citizens of earth to live as though they are citizens of heaven. And they are not buying what we are selling.

Why should we convince the unconverted to permit prayer in public schools? How can we expect them to pray to a God whom they neither know nor love? Our responsibility is not to put prayer back in our public schools but, as Jim Cymbala has said, to put it back in our churches and homes. Remember, God's agenda is the conversion of the heart, not merely the convincing of the mind.

A few years ago I was walking across the temple area in Jerusalem and overheard an argument, in German, as to whether the Muslims, Jews, and Christians all shared the same God or had different Gods. I turned to someone next to me and said, "Well, at least those two men are discussing a question that is much more important than who will win the next presidential election or whether we will be able to save the environment...." In fact, if I had known German well enough I would have tried to enter into the discussion!

The greatest lie in America may be simply stated: it is the belief that each person can come to God in his own way, without a prescribed sacrifice, without a qualified priest, and without blood. This is the lie that we must expose; this is the point that we must address. It is nothing less than defending the uniqueness of Christ in the face of a blizzard of religious options.

When Paul entered the pagan city of Corinth he didn't begin a campaign to clean up the city's morals. He preached Christ crucified, urging his listeners to flee from the city of man to the city of God. Of course Christians should be fighting pornography, gambling, and other moral sins that plague our society. But our first duty is to cleanse the church of these sins. Only then should we endeavor to spread our influence beyond our walls.

In our efforts to change the world we may even appeal to common grace and enlist the help of those of other religions in hopes of shoring up support for our agenda, but let us not confuse such a moralistic campaign with the essence of Christianity. Christianity, properly understood, is the message that God is holy and punishes sin, and if we do not flee to the protection of Christ we will be condemned forever.

A friend of mine was interviewed by a reporter doing a story on the so-called "Christian Right." This journalist interviewed 40 Christians involved in politics—those who are attempting to transform culture with a ballot box. At the end of the interview my friend asked, "Has anyone explained the gospel to you?" The reporter answered, "No, what is the gospel?" She had no idea that this was Christianity's primary message.

Have we forgotten that if there is any good news in America it will not come from Washington, but through the lips of God's people? We cannot evangelize America unless every Christian begins to witness for Christ wherever God has planted him or her.

Using the Right Weapons

Second, we must *use the right weapons*. In America, millions of Christians belong to one or more political organizations that are dedicated to "the Christian agenda." Politics in America is based on a majority vote, and because Christians are a minority, we are told that we have to join with Catholics, Jews, Mormons, and others to fight the evils of our land. I've already implied that there might be some value in such coalitions, and we should be grateful for everyone who sides with believers on such issues as abortion, gambling, homosexual values, and the like. But please hear me when I say that *issues which have such widespread support cannot possibly be the primary mission of the church.*

Some individuals have even gone so far as to suggest that our culture war is so great that we must compromise the doctrine of justification by faith alone in order to gain broader support for our social agenda. But to do that would be to surrender the one weapon we have that can possibly combat the wickedness of this age. We would be sacrificing an eternal message for a temporary one!

Pastor Alistair Begg has correctly pointed out that, in regard to the doctrine of justification, that which divides us from others is much greater than anything that could possibly unite us. Luther was right when he said that it is by this doctrine that the church stands or falls. We are handing the keys to the traitors if we think that we can compromise the one message that can save us in exchange for greater cooperation on moral and political issues.

In Colorado a measure that conservative Christians once hailed as a model for overturning the "gay agenda" backfired when the U.S. Supreme Court, by a 6-3 decision, struck down Amendment 2, which had been approved by voters. The court said that this was a flagrant violation of the Equal Protection Clause in the Fourteenth Amendment to the U.S. Constitution.

Supporters of Amendment 2 expressed concern that the court's decision might be the beginning of the end of individual citizen's rights groups to oppose homosexual activism or even express the opinion that homosexuality is immoral. Will Perkins, who ran the grassroots campaign said, "This decision represents a body blow against freedom of belief and freedom of association." He believes that the court's decision will have far-reaching consequences, hurting the nation's children, setting back the campaign to preserve family values, and opening the door for "a flood of pro-homosexual legal attacks which homosexual extremists will now initiate." Politics is indeed a high-stakes game with inherent risks.

Please understand that I'm not saying we should withdraw from legal battles—particularly those that have to do with freedom of religion. Organizations such as the Rutherford Institute have successfully challenged violations of religious privileges allowed by the First Amendment. However, even freedom of religion can become an idol. The simple fact is that throughout the 2000 years of church history, the church has seldom had freedom of religion. Read the history of the church in Europe, Russia, and China and you will be convinced that *it is not necessary to have freedom in order to be faithful.*

I am not arguing for passivity, nor am I encouraging isolation. Christians have been on the forefront of legislation to pass child labor laws and abolish slavery. We should be on the forefront to protect unborn children from the abortionist's knife. But even here we need to be reminded that a change in the law does not bring about a change in the heart. Only the cross can do that.

When we get involved in such battles, we must remember to use persuasion for promoting our point of view rather than attack-dog political confrontation. And if we form alliances with people from a broad spectrum of religious beliefs, let us not call the organization *Christian.* Let us appeal to compassion and justice, but not draw lines in the sand that force even moderate people to take sides. Thanks to what theologians call *common grace,* we may receive support from people who are not specifically Christian. This is, in my opinion, the proper use of what Francis Schaeffer used to call "co-belligerency."

And if we want to lobby for other matters like the balanced budget amendment, tax breaks for families, or even support for the NRA, then fine, but let us not nail these agendas to the cross as if they are the "Christian" agenda. I grieve because for many observers *the cross of Christ appears to the world as a dilapidated bulletin board cluttered with a whole host of issues!*

We need to rectify our reputation, which has been tarnished by the radicals among us. We can win America only if every single Christian becomes an activist, assuming the delicate task of taking a firm and loving stand on the issues yet presenting spiritual healing to a society that is afflicted with the disease called sin. We are to hold up the cross and display "the excellencies of Him who has called [us] out of darkness into His marvelous light"

(1 Peter 2:9). Believers the world over have proven that living "in Christ" is possible even if the state is antagonistic to the Christian worldview.

The average person will never be convinced of the credibility of the cross until he becomes personally acquainted with someone who lives out the Christian faith, applying its implications to every situation, even at great personal cost. Many Americans have never met someone who is pro-life yet also loves women who have had abortions. They think they have never met anyone who is opposed to the homosexual agenda yet loves homosexuals. They do not know someone who is opposed to sex education and yet is willing to work with the school board to find an alternative. I believe that there are tens of thousands of Christians who have the right perspective, but they have been reduced to silence by the loud din of the media as it smothers us with pro-abortion, pro-homosexual rhetoric. We have been intimidated, but there is much more to our agenda than simply speaking up.

We must bring the cross out of our churches and carry it to a hurting world. Our task is not to save America, but to save Americans by living the gospel. "Keep your behavior excellent among the Gentiles, so that in the thing in which they slander you as evildoers, they may on account of your good deeds, as they observe them, glorify God in the day of visitation" (1 Peter 2:12).

Several times I have stood in the "Luther Stube" in the Wartburg Castle, where, it is said, Luther threw an inkwell at the devil (enterprising tour leaders used to put soot on the wall so as not to disappoint tourists!). But an inkwell thrown at the devil would hardly do the fiend harm; you cannot fight against a spirit with a material weapon!

Perhaps there is a better explanation of what happened in that room. In his Table Talks, Luther said that he "fought the devil with ink." Most likely he meant that he fought the devil through the translation of the New Testament into German, a feat accomplished in that small room in just 11 weeks! What an inkwell thrown at the devil could never accomplish, the Word of God did!

We are constantly in danger of using the wrong weapons because we have incorrectly identified the enemy. Our greatest weapon is not politics (important as politics may be), but the blessed news of the gospel, accurately proclaimed. If we are not careful we will be expecting inkwells to do what only God's Word can do!

Politics is a game of high risk. If you live by the ballot box, you must die by the ballot box. It is a game of numbers in which the majority rules, whether the majority be right or wrong. The question is how we shall live in a culture in which we are outnumbered, even with our coalitions and voting blocs.

To those attempting to revive a nation through politics, Mr. Lewis's demon (in *The Screwtape Letters)* instructs his young charge on how to corrupt his assignment:

> Let him begin by treating the Patriotism as part of his religion. Then let him, under the influence of partisan spirit, come to regard it as the most important part. Then quietly and gradually nurse him on to the state at which the religion becomes merely a part of the "cause," in which Christianity is valued chiefly because of the excellent arguments it can produce.... Once you have made the World an end, and faith a means, you have almost won your man, and it makes very little difference what kind of worldly end he is pursuing.[2]

Having the Right Attitude

Finally, we must *fight with the right attitude*. Of course we must speak up on behalf of unborn infants. Of course we should work together to end racism and bring about just laws. But we must fight with an attitude of humility. We should not approach society and claim that we have all the answers for the escalation of violence and child abuse. We should not pretend that if we were in charge our nation's moral descent would end.

As we call for changes in society we need to exercise caution that we do not lord it over others, or self-righteously point out people's sins. We need to serve knowing that the sins that exist in the world are also found in the church. We need to humbly admit that Luther might have been right when he said, "I would rather be governed by a wise Turk than a stupid Christian."

We need to let go of any illusions that the city of man can become sanctified. We can pray for the city of man as Abraham did for Sodom and Gomorrah, knowing that we have relatives who live within its gates. We can be the first to help the single mother who does not know how she can cope with her baby. We can reach out to homosexual or promiscuous individuals who have AIDS, not with self-righteous condemnation, but with the recognition that we too are sinners who could easily be a part of that lifestyle. We should always judge ourselves more harshly than we judge others.

We cannot take the cross—which should humble us—and turn it into a club in order to make the world "shape up." We are to pursue our primary mission with single-mindedness and heartfelt conviction. We need to remember that America cannot be restored by a change of administrations in Washington, even if there is a "Christian" party. If Luther could not have vanquished the devil by throwing an inkwell at him, neither can we vanquish our foe by the ballot box or in the courts.

We must keep in mind that power corrupts Christians, too. Even those who represent biblical values often compromise their convictions to get re-elected. If we have any doubt as to what effect political power can have on the church, we need look no further than medieval Europe. When the church was in charge, wielding political power and selling political appointments, she became as corrupt as the world she was to reach. We cannot say that fairness, integrity, and moral uprightness have always characterized the times when Christians have taken over the political structure. Of course we should vote for Christians who hold our values, but we must also recognize that they, too, have feet of clay. We've all had our disappointments in those whom we thought would bring about needed political change.

We have a more powerful weapon . . . if only we would use it. More on that later.

The Cross Against the Flag

How should we deal with matters of conscience?

The Roman government to whom the early Christians paid taxes did, as we know, make demands that the Christians could not accept. When the state required them to confess Caesar as Lord, the Christians had to say no to Caesar in order to say yes to God. And when the state forbade them to preach the gospel, they affirmed that they had to "obey God rather than men."

When do we disobey? When we are told to do something that the Bible forbids, or asked to refrain from doing what the Bible commands. If you had lived in East Germany in the sixties and you had been asked to help build the Berlin Wall, you would have complied. But if you had been told that you couldn't share the gospel, you could not have abided by that restriction. You would've had to share the gospel carefully and wisely, but you would have shared it nevertheless. That's because you are called to preach the gospel "to every creature."

What can you do if your children are expected to see steamy sex films in schools as a part of the sex education curriculum? You can go to the teacher and try to resolve the matter. If that doesn't work, you can go to the school board and, if necessary, join a coalition of parents who are willing to protest this violation of parent/child responsibility. You do not want to antagonize others by pronouncing strong words of condemnation or by demonizing those who don't see matters your way. Realize that, by your life and attitude, Christ is on display.

What can we in our churches do when we are told that we will lose our tax-exempt status if we refuse to marry homosexual couples? We can seek to block such legislation, arguing that churches and other charitable organizations of like mind provide valuable services to the community. But we do not call our opponents names; rather, we should hope that reason will prevail. If we want, we can seek the advice of legal experts, but we should not imply that the church, which is built upon Christ, will wither away if tax exemption were denied.

When we disagree, we must do so wisely. Our speech is always to be "seasoned with grace." If a child is forbidden to draw a nativity scene in school, we do not threaten with a court case or lawsuit. We talk to the teacher, to school administrators. We try to work with those who belong to the city of man rather than do anything that will generate needless antagonism.

We must also disagree honestly. We must never misrepresent our adversaries in an attempt to stir people to support our side of the cause. We see this happen in fundraising letters that are sensational, overblown, and intended to make us angry (conventional wisdom says that only angry people send money). Equally foolish is the assumption that the organization that wants our funds is actually in a position to fix whatever has gone wrong!

And, we must disagree humbly. Don't complain when the media is unfair. Our Lord Jesus Christ didn't complain when the soldiers were unfair. We shouldn't castigate the media as if our cause is dependent on their "fair reporting." Why argue with the *Washington Post* about how many attended a pro-life rally? If the paper said 200,000 and we think it is 500,000, so be it. Why should we expect those who are pro-choice to be fair in reporting on a matter about which they have such deeply held beliefs? Have we who are on the other side of this volatile issue always been "fair"?

The Proper Perspective

When it comes to such differences, there are many who often don't act "Christianly" when disagreements arise; why should we expect such behavior from the unconverted? We should not be alarmed if unbelievers act like unbelievers; we should be alarmed, however, when believers act like *un*believers!

We should not see ourselves as the "persecuted minority" and whine about how difficult the world has made things for us. We can only humbly acknowledge that unless God helps us we will not be helped; unless we are redeemed in His grace we shall be lost. We stand with sinners, acknowledging that apart from unmerited grace, we would be where they are today.

Take heart!

It *is* possible for the kingdom of man to decline and the kingdom of God to be doing just fine! In fact, the church has the responsibility of picking up the pieces of a rotting society. Just as everything that has ever been nailed down is torn up, we have the privilege of coming in the name of Christ to people in need.

Missionary experts tell us that the church in China, where vicious persecution has been felt for the past 50 years, has grown more than the church in Taiwan, which has many more freedoms.

I say this not to glorify persecution, but to point out that the success of the city of God is not dependent on the favor of the city of man. We are, after all, pilgrims en route to our permanent home.

Christ never promised it would be easy.

THREE

What God Thinks
of the Cross

Is it realistic to think that our best hope of transforming culture is the power of the gospel? Randall Terry, past leader of Operation Rescue, does not think so. He wrote:

> We have more "gospel preaching" in America than any other nation on earth. Yet America is growing more corrupt by the week; injustice in the courts is growing; oppression against Christians is on the rise; mockery of the holy has become common; homosexuals are demanding to be

married and have children.... All of our gospel preaching hasn't stopped.... a tidal wave that threatens our very survival.... We have more churches, more gospel radio, gospel television, gospel literature, gospel tracts, street meetings, evangelistic crusades, gospel music.... And yet, America is fast becoming the moral cesspool of the earth.[1]

Terry thinks that Christians continue to cling to "an inadequate solution" for this nation's moral and spiritual ills. He cannot understand the inconsistency between the amount of gospel being preached and the meager results being realized. What has gone wrong?

Lest we be tempted to conclude that the gospel is *not* the power of God unto salvation (see Romans 1:16), I would like to suggest that what often passes for the gospel is not really the gospel at all, but rather a message distorted by popular culture. We as evangelicals have been so deeply shaped by the spirit of our age that many of us do not realize that we have bowed to the gods of modernity. The fact is, Terry is wrong about the gospel being widespread in America. Preaching might be widespread, Christian book sales might be on the increase, and the media might be expanding religious programming, but is the gospel really all that widespread in America? I think not.

Just listen to much of the "gospel" preached in America, and you will find the themes of popular culture: a belief in the essential goodness of man, and the goals of happiness, wealth, and health. You will hear a gospel that is rife with stories of miracles based just as much on the power of the human mind as the power of God. You will find a great emphasis on spirituality, personal fulfillment, and openness to other belief systems. What you will not find is a clear proclamation on the depravity of man, the holiness of God, and the urgent need for us to humble ourselves and approach God through Christ's sacrifice alone.

Furthermore, it is simplistic to say that all the ills of society have to be laid at the door of the church. Certainly we have not been all that we should be; most assuredly, the church has lost much of its credibility in the world. But never in history has a society as a whole embraced the distinctive Christian message that Christ died for sinners, accepting Him as Lord and Savior.

Surely we would not want to say that if only Christ had prayed more, or preached better sermons, the city of Jerusalem would have accepted Him as Messiah. God has His hidden purposes even in the judgment of a corrupt culture. Contrary to much popular theology, the future of America does not rest with us, but with the sovereign purposes of God.

The Apostles and the Cross

That said, we can take heart knowing that this is not the first time the church has been in a decidedly minority position in the world. The apostles found themselves up against a social, political, and religious barrier that they could not move. They had no political appointments, no judgeships, and no freedom to properly voice their frustrations.

And yet they turned the world upside down.

Read what Peter said to his antagonists after he had been released from a Jerusalem prison: "There is salvation in no one else; for there is no other name under heaven that has been given among men, by which we must be saved" (Acts 4:12).

The bleak political circumstances of that age did not shake Peter's confidence in God, nor did it deter the disciples from getting the message out. There was joy in the face of persecution and political uncertainty. The apostles seemed blissfully oblivious to the barriers that surrounded them; they were convinced that the message Christ gave them could not be suppressed by the authorities of that day. Neither did they naively think that everyone would become a believer. The fact that Christ promised them persecution is reason enough to show that they did not think the preaching of the gospel would bring about some kind of a Christian utopia.

The apostles were, however, motivated by the deep conviction that God had entered their world; they had a message that could grip the heart of the most notorious sinner. This confidence gave them an impact on society that was much greater than their numbers might suggest. Faced with ridicule, ostracism, and persecution, they kept the main thing the main thing. Even if no one had believed, they would have continued to do God's work, leaving the results in His hands.

If the cross is at the heart of God's agenda, it most assuredly should be at the heart of ours as well. And when I speak of the cross, I do not refer to a piece of wood upon which Christ died, but the death itself—and not just the death, but His resurrection and ascension.

The cross is the hinge on which the door of history swings; it is the hub that holds the spokes of God's purposes. The Old Testament prophets pointed toward it and the New Testament prophets proclaimed it. And, properly understood, it is even today "the power of God unto salvation." When we "cling to that old rugged cross" as the old but familiar song encourages us to do, we are not doing so out of mere sentimentality. The cross is the heart of our message and the heart of our power to combat the encroaching darkness.

God has chosen this world to be the stage on which a drama would unfold. Here on this planet the issues of justice and injustice, truth and error, kindness and cruelty are being fought. God and the devil are pitted against each other, and thankfully there is no doubt about the outcome. God is the scriptwriter and He supervises this cosmic play, making sure it will turn out as planned. And His script was written long ago.

Come with me on a journey into the mind of God; we will encounter some challenging ideas, and when we are finished we will see our own political/cultural conflicts in a new light. Looked at from the panorama of eternity, we will be encouraged to stay on target.

The Cross in God's Heart

How long has the cross been a part of God's plan?

After Adam and Eve sinned, God told the serpent, "I will put enmity between you and the woman, and between your seed and her seed; he shall bruise you on the head, and you shall bruise him on the heel" (Genesis 3:15). God promised He would take the initiative: "I will…." He also predicted that the redemption of man would involve suffering—"enmity" would be the order of the day. And, thankfully, the seed of the woman (Christ) would crush the head of the serpent.

When did this plan form in God's mind? Was He actually expecting, perhaps hoping, that Adam and Eve would obey His command so that they would live in perpetual bliss? Or was the redemption available through the cross in His mind long before Eve was mesmerized by the beautiful fruit of the forbidden tree? There are three possible answers.

The first is to say that the plan to redeem man became a part of God's agenda when our first parents stood amid the ruins of paradise. Then and there He graciously concluded that He would do something about their predicament.

God, some have taught, had high hopes for Adam and Eve, but they disappointed Him, so He turned to another plan. In fact, one evangelical pastor, in a message titled, "God the Gambler," said that God gambled on His creation, betting that they would serve Him. When He lost the gamble and Adam and Eve sinned, He did what any gambler does: He upped the ante, and bet His Son. This pastor actually quoted John 3:16 to read, "For God so loved the world that He *bet* His only begotten Son...."

For this minister, if we dare call him such, there were no guarantees; God had no assurance that anyone would believe on Christ after He died for sinners. After all, because of "free will," it was conceivable that no one would believe on Christ. God could have lost the whole gamble!

According to this scenario, the death of Christ was God's response to an emergency He was hoping would not happen. We can be grateful that God came to clean up the mess, but He lost the gamble. Nothing about His plans was certain. Yet because God is loving, He can be expected to do whatever He can to help us.

Should we wonder why the gospel proclaimed from some pulpits today is unable to save sinners? Because this view is unworthy of God, it is also unworthy of further comment.

Second, there are those who say that the idea of the cross was agreed upon at some point before the foundation of the world. Because the Father loves the Son, He agreed to give Him a community of redeemed humanity. And God the Spirit would be the agent by which this gift of redemption would be mediated to mankind. Thus there was a point at which the covenant was ratified, agreed to, and sealed.

Several Scriptures teach that there was such an agreement. Paul wrote to Titus about "eternal life, which God, who cannot lie, promised long ages ago" (1:2). This promise made before the foundation of the world was an agreement made by the members of the Trinity. While on earth, Christ repeatedly referred to the elect as those whom God had given to Him. They are the ones who are a part of the eternal plan of redemption.

This view is of course an immeasurably improved understanding of the cross in God's eternal purpose. God's dignity and sovereignty is restored to its rightful place in the scheme of redemption.

But I want to carry the logic one step further and assert that the cross was always in the mind of God, even from the distant aeons of eternity. To put it more clearly, I believe that the plan of redemption is as eternal as God. It makes no more sense to ask, "When did the idea of the cross have its beginning?" than it would be to ask, "When did God have a beginning?" As long as there was God, there was the cross in His heart.

There are two reasons I say this:

First, because God never learns anything. In fact, we can say that all of God's decisions were already known to Him as long as He has existed, and that is forever. We should never think that at any time God did not quite know what to do, so He wrestled with the problem and later "made up His mind." As a friend of mine used to ask, "Has it ever dawned on you that nothing has ever dawned on God?"

Though all of God's works have been known to Him from all of eternity, the cross was the focal point of His program. In redemption His attributes would be most clearly displayed.

Second, if you still doubt that the cross is as eternal as God, consider the words of Paul: "...God, who has saved us, and called us with a holy calling, not according to our works, but according to His own purpose and grace which was granted us in Christ Jesus from all eternity" (2 Timothy 1:8,9). Literally the original Greek text reads that grace was granted to us "before the ages of eternity"!

We must pause to catch our breath. I, for one, cannot understand how God can have eternally existed. I can understand eternity future, but not eternity past. As the saying goes, we can't "get our mind around" such a concept. Yet however much we struggle with the fact that God had no beginning, we can rejoice that the redeemed have been known to Him as long as He has existed! Already back then it was certain that they would be granted grace! To put it differently, if you are redeemed, there never was a time when you were not already loved by God; there never was a time when you were not the object of His specific purpose. That is why John could say that our names were written in the Lamb's book of life "from the foundation of the world" (Revelation 13:8).

In regard to Paul's statement that God chose us in Christ from "before the foundation of the world" (Ephesians 1:4), we are evidently not to think that there was a specific point before creation that we were chosen; rather, the choice was as eternal as God. We were chosen, yes, but the choice has existed as long as God has existed. Given the difficulty of comprehending eternity past, it is quite understandable that we speak of God as choosing, willing, and planning at some point before creation. We struggle with the idea that the script God wrote for the universe has existed as long as He has. What is important is that we realize there was a cross in God's heart long before there was a cross raised upon the Mount of Calvary. There was no gamble here.

If you or someone you know is troubled, wondering whether he or she is among this chosen company, keep in mind that we can find out whether we are among "the elect." All we must do is come to Christ, transferring our trust to Him alone. When we do that, it is proof that we are included in the number of the redeemed—those to whom grace has been shown "from all eternity." Indeed, the invitation is to whoever is willing to come.

God wants to be known by His creation as a redeeming God. To accomplish this, the scripted drama had to become a reality on earth. And it is unthinkable that His eternal plan will fail.

Remember, the real story is God's redemptive history, not the fluc-tuating ebb and flow of the kingdoms of this world.

The Cross in History

God's plan called for Christ's death. How was this to be brought about?

A coalition of God's enemies would conspire together to put Christ to death. Evil men would set aside their differences and concentrate on the one man they hated the most. Christ would be neutralized; He would be taken out of the way so that men could continue in their sins without rebuke or irritation. Peter explained it this way: "Truly in this city there were gathered together against Thy holy servant Jesus, whom Thou didst anoint, both Herod and Pontius Pilate, along with the Gentiles and the peoples of Israel, to do whatever Thy hand and Thy purpose *predestined* to occur" (Acts 4:27,28, emphasis added). These were the players on the stage when Christ offered Himself to the people as their redeemer.

Herod Antipas was the ruler of Galilee; he was the man who murdered John the Baptist. Herod was probably quite surprised and uncertain when the guards brought Jesus to him. But the more Herod questioned Jesus the bolder he became, even suggesting that Christ entertain him with a miracle! Christ responded by saying nothing. As Warren Wiersbe said, Herod silenced the voice of God! Yet it was not Herod who was judging Jesus; rather, it was Jesus who was judging Herod.

Herod mocked Christ and permitted the soldiers to dress him in an elegant robe. He did not issue a final verdict about Jesus, but it was clear that he did not find Jesus worthy of death. And yet, he was glad to see Him die. Flagrant injustice!

Pontius Pilate was another player on the stage. He will always be remembered as a tragic figure; he knew that Christ was innocent and even wanted to see Him released. But in the end, Pilate handed Jesus over to the mob. Pilate's wife, bless her, warned her husband to have nothing to do with Jesus because of a terrifying dream she had the previous night. Pilate, wanting desperately to take his wife's advice, suggested to the people that Christ be set free in accordance with their custom of releasing a prisoner during the Passover. He wanted to flog Jesus and let Him go. But the mob shouted, "Release unto us Barabbas!" As for Christ, they shouted, "Crucify Him! Crucify Him!"

Pilate washed his hands to signify that he wanted nothing to do with the condemnation of this innocent man. And yet faced with the screaming mob, and wanting to maintain a favorable status with the Jews, he granted their request. Today he is remembered not for his leadership among the Jews, but for his cowardice.

Interestingly, Pilate and Herod were enemies, each vying for a privileged position in the Roman pecking order. But Christ united them. On that very day, we read, they "became friends" (Luke 23:12). Sometimes old animosities have to be set aside to execute a common enemy.

Next, Peter mentions the Gentiles—that is, the Romans who actually carried out the crucifixion. They were, for the most part, indifferent to the squabbles that the Jews had with Jesus. The Romans occupied this region primarily for the purpose of keeping order. But they also wanted to please the Jews whenever they could, hence they upheld the verdict of the Jewish courts. If the authorities wanted Christ to be crucified, so be it.

Finally, Peter mentions the "peoples of Israel"—the religious leaders who had become weary of answering questions about Christ. Though they wanted Christ killed on the grounds of blasphemy, their underlying motive was not theological. Pilate, who had his ear to the ground and who was a keen observer of human nature, knew that it was "because of envy that they had delivered

Him up" (Matthew 27:18). Put simply, Christ made the religious leaders look bad. Christ had the crowds and the charisma; He had the authority and the power.

These are the players on the stage of history who conspired to put Christ to death. Was there any chance that they would do otherwise? Did God gamble that His Son would actually be killed? Hardly. Peter explains that these people gathered together "to do whatever Thy hand and Thy purpose predestined to occur" (Acts 4:28). God saw to it that there was no possibility that His plan would fail. The wicked would do what God marked out beforehand; Christ would die and His death would provide salvation for all who would believe. When man did his worst, God would do His best.

Indeed, the very hour that Christ died was predetermined. In Old Testament times the Passover lamb was slain "between the evenings," according to the Hebrew text. Tradition said that this was somewhere in the three-hour period between 3:00 and 6:00 P.M. Notice that it was between these hours that Christ became our sin-bearer on that Passover day in Jerusalem: "And about the ninth hour [3:00 P.M.] Jesus cried out with a loud voice, saying 'Eli, Eli, lama sabachthani?' that is, 'My God, My God, why hast Thou forsaken Me?' " (Matthew 27:46). He died on the right day at the right time, just as God had planned.

That word "predestined" in Acts 4:28 simply means "to predetermine." If God predetermined that these men would collaborate in having Christ put to death, did they have any choice in the matter? As players on this cosmic stage, were they simply puppets on a string, obediently playing their scripts? Needless to say, this is not the place to discuss all of these mysteries. We must read the Bible accepting both of these premises: first, that men act voluntarily— they do as they wish, and thus they are responsible. And second,

God, through secondary causes, guides the course of history so that it unravels according to His will.

If we could have interviewed Herod to ask him why he did not defend Christ, he would not have answered, "Because I felt the pressure of a divine decree." No, he did as he pleased. And yet in so doing he was carrying out what God predestined to occur. The same can be said for the other conspirators.

The question is not whether predestination is agreeable to us, but whether God has revealed it. Obviously, a study of this doctrine is beyond the scope and intention of this book. My purpose in quoting Peter is simply to point out that God's purposes are sure and cannot fail. When Paul was countering the prevailing notion that God's purposes were floundering because the Jews did not believe, he answered, "It is not as though the word of God has failed. For they are not all Israel who are descended from Israel" (Romans 9:6). Then he goes on to show that the elect are being saved—thus God's purposes are on target.

Of course some people object to teaching the total sovereignty of God, arguing that it leads to fatalism; there are probably many examples of this historically. However, if we were to ask Luther, Calvin, or Edwards about the matter, they would say that it is this doctrine that gives us hope in the midst of the doctrinal decay all around us.

If you wonder what this has to do with the preaching of the gospel in America today, it is simply this: Until we understand and preach the doctrine of man's inability to contribute to his salvation, we will always preach a gospel that falls short of the helpless dependence upon God that should characterize our witness. We will be satisfied with calling people to Christ without them understanding how desperately they really need Him. Christ will be seen as the remedy for "peace and happiness" rather than the grounds of a sinner's justification before God. Given the kind of gospel preached in our pulpits, we should not be surprised that the message has lost its power.

Would that Christians in America would see the great barrier that God must overcome in saving a sinner! We can do no better than to read these words from the great English preacher Charles Haddon Spurgeon:

> I shall not attempt to teach a tiger the virtues of vegetarianism; but I shall as hopefully attempt that task as I would try to convince an unregenerate man of the truths revealed by God concerning sin, and righteousness and judgment to come. These spiritual truths are repugnant to carnal men, and the carnal mind cannot receive the things of God. Gospel truth is diametrically opposed to fallen nature; and if I have not a power much stronger than that which lies in moral suasion [persuasion], or in my own explanations and arguments, I have undertaken a task in which I am sure of defeat.... Except the Lord endow us with power from on high, our labour must be in vain, and our hopes must end in disappointment.[2]

Our responsibility is to be true to the message that God, in His gracious mercy, might be pleased to bless. We must exalt the cross since it is there that our salvation was purchased; it is there that God set forth Christ publicly to display His righteousness (Romans 3:25). God wants to demonstrate that His compassion will never cause him to overlook sin. He must prove that He is just, though He is also "the justifier of the one who has faith in Jesus" (Romans 3:26). God set forth Christ to defend His integrity.

The doctrine of justification teaches that God is now free to declare sinners as righteous as He Himself is. Indeed, we are credited with the righteousness of Christ. Twenty-four hours a day God demands perfection from His people; 24 hours a day, Christ supplies what God demands. When Luther came to understand this truth, he almost immediately dropped the doctrine of purgatory, which taught that few—if any—die righteous enough to enter heaven. Thanks to God, we are *even now* righteous enough to be brought into the very throne room of the Almighty.

At the cross, the love of God was also displayed. After all, God could have kept His justice intact, even if Christ had not come to redeem us. It was not logically necessary that Christ die; the necessity of the cross was based on the compelling power of love. As we shall see more fully in the next chapter, the wisdom of God was on display at the cross. The dilemma of how sinful human beings could be reconciled to God could not be resolved apart from the divine plan. The cross that was in God's heart became a reality in history.

And yet we shall also see the cross in the future!

The Cross in Heaven

Some people claim to have peered into heaven only to return and tell us what they have seen. These near-death experiences are most assuredly unreliable and even misleading. Certainly some believers, like Stephen, have had the privilege of looking into heaven before they died, but Satan would like to give the same positive experience to unbelievers, too. Thankfully, some reports are reliable, such as the one from John the apostle.

John was not near death but very much alive when he was given a glimpse into heaven. He wrote, "After these things I looked, and behold, a door standing open in heaven…" (Revelation 4:1). There he saw God on the throne, and heard the worship of the creatures who surrounded Him. He also saw a scroll, a script that recorded the last years of the history of this world. An angel was proclaiming with a loud voice, "Who is worthy to open the book and to break its seals?" (Revelation 5:2).

John wept because at first it appeared as if no one had the authority to open the scroll. But he was told to stop weeping, for the Lion of the tribe of Judah was worthy to open the scroll, read the script, and make sure it was followed. John wrote, "I saw between the throne (with the four living creatures) and the elders a Lamb standing, *as if slain,* having seven horns and seven eyes, which are the seven Spirits of God, sent out into all the earth" (verse 6).

The cross in heaven!

Just as the body of the resurrected Christ had the print of the nails and the scar of the wounded side, so this lamb appears "as if slain." Far from being an event in the past, the marks of the cross of Christ are found in the center of heaven itself. The cross, someone has observed, changed the unchangeable! Heaven itself is different, for when the Lamb appeared, "they sang a new song" (verse 9).

Notice the lyrics: "Worthy art Thou to take the book, and to break its seals; for Thou wast slain, and didst purchase for God with Thy blood men from every tribe and tongue and people and nation" (verse 9). If it were not for the cross, the people mentioned in that verse would not be in heaven. These who have been the objects of God's love for as long as He has existed can rejoice! Some have already made their safe arrival in heaven, others of us are en route. All of us can rejoice because we have been made a kingdom of priests and we will reign on the earth. Ours is a kingdom that will not be shaken, a kingdom that is unaffected by the chaos that exists on the earth.

"It is not what you know, but who you know that matters," we are often told. If this is true on earth, think of how much more it is true in heaven. It is those who know the Lamb who are most blessed. They have the heavenly city to look forward to—a city that will usher them into eternity, separated from the city of man forever.

Revisiting the Cross and the Flag

What conclusions can we draw from the primacy of the cross in God's program?

First, *spiritual redemption, not political reformation, is at the heart of God's agenda.* The closer we get to the cross, the closer we get to His heart. Here we see God at His "best."

Once we understand the cross we cannot be satisfied with the civil religion of former president Dwight Eisenhower, who was fond of saying, "Our government makes no sense unless it is founded on a deeply felt religious faith—*and I don't care what it is*"[3] (emphasis added). No, we are not commissioned to call America back to God and religion; we are commanded to call America to God through Christ, who died for sinners. Just any religion will not do; just any path to God will not do.

We should never let the earthly kingdom eclipse the eternal one. We dare not pin our hopes on a fading political process, no matter how promising the reforms and the possibility of genuine, positive change. Yes, of course we are left here to make the world better, but more important, we are left here to make heaven complete. Of course our task is more difficult than convincing a tiger of the benefits of vegetarianism, but that is why we must trust God to overcome the blindness of the human heart and grant men and women the ability to believe.

I wonder if those who think that our best hope is political muscle, lobbying, protests, and letter-writing campaigns have ever taken the time to study how Christ and His disciples turned their world upside down. We have something so precious that nothing should ever get in the way of our primary mission. How dare we be satisfied with our moral and political strategies—our message is more radical, more urgent!

The early Christians knew their agenda. Though beaten, they continued in boldness. They never questioned the power of the cross to both save and deliver people from their sins. Yes, we might become discouraged when we see people who profess faith and yet do not follow through. And we have all committed enough sins to make us doubt the power of God. But the cross stands as a constant reminder of our great need and God's great grace.

Second, *God's agenda includes all nations, not just one special nation.* There is no special place in heaven for Americans. God desires to have a transnational community. His plan for this cosmos is so much greater than the preservation of the American dream. He desires that there be people redeemed from Asia, Africa, South America, and the Middle East. God's plan is as great as our world.

Third, *the church, not a political party, is the bearer of God's message.* We creatively use our lives to develop credibility because we know that the power of the gospel is not just in the words we speak but in the lives we live. When Christ said we are the light of the world and the salt of the earth, He did not mean that we are to change the world through politics. Our danger is that we might get used to the darkness rather than let our lights shine even more brightly.

Columnist Cal Thomas recently editorialized about the Christian Coalition and the retirement of its executive director, Ralph Reed, by reminding us of the church's real purpose in this present age:

> When Christian activists moved into the political arena, they targeted pornography, offensive television, drugs, the gay rights movement and crumbling families. Pornography is worse than ever, television continues to stink, drugs

remain a problem, the gay-rights agenda advances and the divorce rate remains about the same.

… conservative evangelicals run the risk of depreciating their ultimate value, that of speaking of and building a kingdom "not of this world." There is precedent for what happens to the church's primary witness when it becomes overly entangled in the cares of this world. Look at the liberal churches, which long ago gave up preaching salvation and now mainly focus on political themes.

Christians have strayed too far from their leader's admonition to "love your enemies; pray for those who persecute you; feed the hungry, clothe the naked and visit those in prison." Clearly, the Christian Coalition's attempt to organize a minority constituency to influence a majority who do not share their views is not working (otherwise, our culture would not have declined to the point it has). Suppose the coalition became known for transforming people's lives instead of trying to transform Congress and the White House? Might it be argued that their example would be so compelling that millions of Americans would follow it?

Conservative Christians claim that by force of numbers alone, which they do not have, they can redeem a culture gone sour. It won't happen through the ballot box, no matter who is elected. It can happen only through the heart.

C.S. Lewis put it bluntly: "If you read history, you will find that the Christians who did the most for the present world were just those who thought most of the next. The apostles, themselves, who set on foot the conversion of the Roman Empire, the great men who built up the Middle Ages, the English evangelicals who abolished the slave trade, all left their mark on earth, precisely because their minds were occupied with heaven. It is since Christians have largely ceased to think of the other world that they have become so ineffective in this one. Aim at heaven and you will get earth 'thrown in.' Aim at earth and you will get neither."[4]

When the moral and spiritual decline of England seemed irreversible, God raised up John Wesley to preach the gospel. During those days the British Parliament sometimes had to disband at midday because the members were too drunk to continue deliberations. Children worked in factories, rejected and exploited. The revival of the eighteenth century changed that. The transformation of heart brought a transformation of country. We do not know if God will do the same for America. Clearly we do not deserve it, nor can we insist that He give it to us because "we are His special nation." But perhaps if we confessed our sin of depending on our own clout and turned to Him alone, He might yet be gracious to us, even in this late hour.

When the world was exceedingly wicked, there was Noah.

When the knowledge of the Lord was obliterated from the earth, there was Abraham.

When the chosen people were weary with bondage, there was Moses.

When New England was turning away from God, there was Jonathan Edwards.

When Augustine was told that Rome had been looted by the barbarians, he said, "Whatever men build, men will destroy. Let's get on with the business of building the kingdom of God."

Yes, whatever men build, men will destroy. With that in mind, let's remember this Scripture: "Since we receive a kingdom which cannot be shaken, let us show gratitude, by which we may offer to God an acceptable service with reverence and awe; for our God is a consuming fire" (Hebrews 12:28,29).

When we stay close to the cross, we are close to God's heart. When we are close to God's heart, we are close to God's power. And when we are close to God's power, we are close to lighting the darkness. Even a candle can cause the darkness in a cave to vanish. The greater the darkness, the more candles that are needed—to share the message of the gospel, to rekindle our belief that it is the power of God unto salvation.

The Consequence of Neglect

Come with me to Stuttgart, Germany, with the nation lying in ruins and Hitler about to commit suicide. Helmut Thielicke, a German pastor and theologian, speaks movingly to his congregation, assessing what has gone wrong. In his powerful critique, he explains that the nation had, in effect, gotten what it deserved because it had "repudiated forgiveness and kicked down the cross of the Lord." Because the cross had been neglected, Germans became blinded, thinking they were special people to God and forgetting that the fist of God had already been raised to "dash them to the ground." The church had concentrated on political and social problems and overlooked its need for a Redeemer "who would set straight the deepest need of their lives."

Then Thielicke came to the heart of the matter:

> Denying God and casting down the cross is never merely a private decision that concerns only my own inner life and my personal salvation, but this denial immediately brings the most brutal consequences for the whole of historical life and especially for our own people. "God is not mocked." The history of the world can tell us terrible tales based on that text.[5]

Germany's greatest problem was not political, but spiritual; it was not just that their leader was perverse, but that the people, for the most part, did not look beyond the earthly kingdom to the heavenly one. There was no political answer to Hitler's atrocities, but there was a spiritual one. He could not be elected out of office, but his orders could have been defied by those who believed that heaven was more important then earth.

Casting down the cross of Christ! For that the church and the country was "crushed by God." Many pastors caved in to the political agenda of the day and refused to preach the cross in their ministries. The congregations fell in step, shielding their eyes from the atrocities around them because they refused to humble themselves at the foot of the cross and take that cross into the world. It is not too strong to say that the failure of many of the German churches can be traced to the loss of the gospel in their life and witness.

Randall Terry is wrong—the gospel is not an "inadequate solution." It might not be the solution to all of America's ills, for even redeemed sinners are yet sinners. The gospel might not speak to every issue on our cultural agenda, or may not look as attractive as the self-help remedies that abound. But it is the only message that can speak to man's greatest and eternal need. If only we understood it better and had the passion to proclaim it more clearly!

FOUR

What Man Thinks
of the Cross

I enjoy taking advantage of the opportunity to share the Good News with people who sit next to me on an airplane. Almost always the conversation turns from politics, to religion, to Christ.

Recently my wife and I were sitting together when I noticed that the woman across the aisle from me was wearing a necklace with a cross. Hoping to stimulate a discussion, I said to her, "Thanks for wearing that cross ... we do have a wonderful Savior, don't we?"

Surprised, she rolled her eyes upward and responded, "Well, I don't think that I understand the cross like you do ... look at this." She held the small cross in her hand and showed me that beneath it was a Jewish Star of David, and beneath that was a trinket that symbolized the Hindu god Om. "I'm in social work. The people I work with find God in different ways ... Christianity is but one of the paths to the divine," she explained.

You can imagine the lively discussion we had for the next 20 minutes on whether the cross can be combined with the other religions of the world. I explained that the cross can be united with other religious symbols on a necklace, but never in reality. The better she understood the cross, the more clearly she saw that it would of necessity have to stand alone; to combine it with a pendant of some other god was to destroy its meaning. We can't come to God in "our own way."

Representing the Cross Rightly

At a time when the message of the cross is greatly needed, the evangelical church, has, for the most part, lost its nerve. In order to not offend the "seekers" who visit our churches, we have hewn the rough edges of the cross to fit the spirit of the age. Some pastors say openly that they will not preach on the holiness of God, the depravity of man, and the exclusivity of the gospel message— for fear of erecting unnecessary stumbling blocks for those who are investigating Christianity. As Robert Schuller put it, "Just because it is in the Bible does not mean that you have to preach it."

But if it is in the Bible, we *must* preach it! To rid the cross (and the cluster of doctrines that surround it) from its "offense" is to rid it of its power. This is precisely the reason why we have so much "gospel" preaching but so little evidence of permanent change in the lives of our hearers.

Our task in this world is both simple and profound: it is to explain the meaning of the cross to a generation that is steeped in Designer Religion; an age in which people think they can find their very own private ways to God. We have to take a message, derided as "sectarian" by the masses, and show why it contains the best news that a person could ever know. Our goal is to take people who despise the cross and share with them its message of love. We are to show why the cross is the great divide—the fork in the road that separates the human race into two groups forever.

Friedrich Nietzsche, a German philosopher of the late nineteenth century, derided Christianity as being weak. He said that qualities such as meekness, pity, and love stood in the way of power, crushing control, and the need for a "Superman." He argued that it wasn't the meek who would inherit the earth, but the ruthless and the mighty. For him, Christ on the cross was just one more sign of weakness, failure, and a *catastrophe*, to use his word. He did not grasp the meaning of Paul's words "the weakness of God is stronger than men" (1 Corinthians 1:25).

It is a scandal beyond irony that men despise what God honors. He values the cross and men dishonor it. At the cross the wisdom of God and the wisdom of man collide. On the one hand are those who glory in it; on the other are those who are embarrassed by it. What the redeemed love, the world ignores and stoutly rejects.

Unfortunately, for many people, the only cross many people carry is one that can be worn as jewelry around the neck or wrist. They are blind to the many victories Christ won while being crucified "in weakness." Someone has said that in Christ's paradoxical new order, everything appears upside-down to the world. Jesus invites us to follow Him in a society where losers are winners, the first are last, and, contrary to Nietzsche, the meek—not the powerful—inherit the earth.

One test of a true church is whether it preaches a message that offends some people. The great seduction before us is to make the message of the cross compatible with culture. Yet to remove its stigma is to remove its power. Let us rediscover a theology of the cross that will take us back to the primary agenda of the church:

> The word of the cross is to those who are perishing foolishness, but to us who are being saved it is the power of God. . . . For since in the wisdom of God the world through its wisdom did not come to know God, God was well-pleased through the foolishness of the message preached to save those who believe (1 Corinthians 1:18,21).

Why does human wisdom fare so poorly next to the cross? Mankind, as we know, is brilliant—the inventor of computers, satellites, and space missions. But when man leaves the empirical world of science and begins to speculate about that which is unseen, he simply does not have the building blocks on which to build a system of knowledge, as proven by the fact that modern philosophy has drifted into skepticism. Given our limitations, we stumble when we attempt to reason from the creation to the creator. Human speculation about God and our relationship to Him is subject to grave error.

The human mind, then, is limited, but we are also misled by the powerful desires of the human heart. We don't even live up to what we know in those matters where reason can give us some specific guidance. Almost always we live by our desires rather than our minds; our minds become the servants of our desires and lusts. The human mind, it has been said, can rationalize anything the human heart wants to do. And today these rationalizations are more clever than ever.

The pagans around us actually believe that they are being guided by human reason. But my observation has been that this is not true: The unconverted I know are driven by their desires and use their reasoning powers to justify what they want to do. Many people behave contrary to both natural law and rational considerations, but have convinced themselves that they are quite fine. They come armed with a whole raft of arguments to "prove" that what they are doing is "right for them."

Although the law of God is written on every human heart, our fallenness stands in the way of coming to know Him. What is more, until the barrier of sin has been set aside, even knowledge based on the Bible is at best purely intellectual and speculative. Meanwhile we are free to live by our own rules, until we are gripped by the reality of the cross.

No matter how skewed the knowledge of the unbeliever, driven by unaided reason and base desires, he is puffed up by what he knows, confident that he does not need a special word from God—much less does He need God's special intervention. And only the message of the cross will tell him otherwise. Only by hearing what he doesn't like to hear can he be reconciled to God, converted, and made a member of God's family. Jesus submitted Himself to weakness and death so that those who are weak and dead might be raised to life.

We must not be discouraged with Paul's dire assessment of human wisdom. It is precisely when we are willing to share a message which is offensive that God's power is activated. Indeed, this is the only message that can shine a light on the blindness of people's hearts. We do not have to dress it up in contemporary garb to make it more presentable. When it is shared in both its horror and its glory, man is given hope.

The better we understand what man thinks of the cross, the better we will be able to present its message to our generation.

Far from this being just a depressing exposition of man's sinfulness, it gives people a window into the heart of God. And it helps to clarify the gospel for those who think that the cross of Christ can be comfortably worn with the pendant of a pagan deity.

The Jews and Greeks to whom Paul refers in 1 Corinthians 1:22,23 are representative of our culture. Here we have a diagnosis of the human heart along with God's wondrous cure.

Our Response to the Cross

The Cross, an Offense to Our Pride

In the Old Testament there is a story about Naaman, a Syrian army captain who had won great military victories. Though he was a valiant warrior, he was also a leper. At the suggestion of a Jewish girl, he made contact with Elisha the prophet, hoping to be healed. Elisha was glad to meet with this high-ranking officer, and gave him a prescription for healing: "Go and wash in the Jordan seven times and your flesh shall be restored to you and you shall be clean" (2 Kings 5:10).

Naaman was insulted. He thought that the prophet would just heal him with the wave of his hand. He added that there were rivers in Damascus (his home territory) that were much cleaner than the Jordan, so he left in a huff. Only because of the persuasion of his servants did he turn back and do what he was told. After a humiliating series of baths in the Jordan, he was healed.

Just so, when we present the message of the cross to people, they are often initially offended. They are glad to know about God's forgiveness, but they are offended when we say that the only basis of forgiveness is the suffering and death of Christ on the cross. Are there not other ways to God that are more akin to our natural talents and gifts? Why such narrow-mindedness? The cross has always been a stumbling block to human under-standing.

Christ clashed with the Pharisees because He represented an entirely different view of Messiahship than that which the Jews wanted. The Jews were scandalized because of the cross, because Jesus did not meet their expectations. Paul put it this way: "Jews ask for signs, and Greeks search for wisdom; but we preach Christ crucified, to the Jews a stumbling block, and to Gentiles foolish-ness" (1 Corinthians 1:22,23).

The Jews were among the first to be offended by the perceived weakness of Christ; the very sight of Him dying in apparent help-lessness was proof positive He was not the man they were looking for. They remembered the words of Deuteronomy, "Anyone who is hung on a tree is under God's curse" (Deuteronomy 21:23 NIV). There was Christ, dying defeated and cursed. The cross, from the Jews' perspective, proved that Jesus was not the Messiah.

They pictured the true Messiah as a military ruler who would finally put an end to the Roman occupation of their land. They were weary of high taxes and the humiliation of servitude. They believed that every denarius paid to these pagans was an offense to Jehovah. After all, the Jews were the people of God; it was an insult for them and for Jehovah to listen to the curses that the Romans heaped upon their nation. Every lash of a whip on a Jewish back, every act of treason at the hands of the Romans, led the Jews to seek for a Messiah who would deliver them from their enemies.

Initially the Jews found themselves attracted to Christ. His miracles intrigued them. But when the crowds followed Him and He claimed to be God, the Jewish religious leaders became angry. Politically Christ was an embarrassment; religiously He was a threat; practically He was useless.

"My kingdom is not of this world," He taught. These were hardly encouraging words for a nation weary of not seeing the Old Testament promises of a glorious kingdom fulfilled. And now He was on the cross! He should have been killing the Romans, and now the Romans were killing Him! He should have been standing tall, but here He was, bowing low. This was not the Messiah sent from God!

No one wants to be associated with a loser.

If you asked the Jews of Christ's day why they did not accept Him as Messiah they might simply say, "He did not perform for us!" They were constantly seeking a sign, some glorious miracle, that would convince them that the Messiah had come. In A.D. 45, a few years after Christ's crucifixion, a man called Theudas persuaded thousands of people to come to the Jordan River, promising them that at his command the waters would divide and he would lead them on dry ground to the other side. Later another would-be Messiah brought 30,000 people to the top of the Mount of Olives with the promise that at his command the walls of Jerusalem would collapse.

If only Christ had done such wonders! If only He had galvanized the Jewish nation against the Romans and led them to deliverance! But when they pestered Him for such a miracle, He sadly replied, "Unless you people see signs and wonders, you simply will not believe" (Romans 4:48).

It has always been so. During the Reformation, official Christendom insisted that the Reformers could not possibly have the true gospel because they did not perform miracles. Rome claimed that it had statues that wept and relics that multiplied all by themselves. So they taunted the Reformers, "Where are your signs?"

As it was then, so it is today. Many people insist that we need signs and wonders to present the gospel to this generation. If we could heal the sick, divert tornadoes, and raise the dead, then this generation would believe. But just as in Christ's day, miracle seekers are never satisfied; there is always one more miracle necessary, one greater than the last. Someone once said that Jesus did miracles but didn't advertise them. Some people today advertise them but don't do them!

My recollection is that when Billy Graham was in India many years ago a Hindu priest challenged him to a "healing duel." The object, evidently, was to see who could heal the most people in the time allotted. Or, perhaps it was to see who could heal the person who was most obviously in need. Either way, Mr. Graham wisely declined.

The apostle Paul believed that the message of the gospel contained within itself "the power of God for salvation" (Romans 1:16). We do not need to compete with New Agers, who give their clients courses in miracles. We do not have to send money to televangelists so that they can bury our names in a jar on the Mount of Olives. We can believe in miracles, but should not be seduced by the fleshly desire to see a sign.

My wife, Rebecca, was a secretary to a man who said, "If I die and find out that there is a God, I'll say to him, 'Well, where have you been?'" God's answer is, "I entered your planet in the person of Christ. I was raised from the dead and ascended into heaven."

That is great enough of a miracle for those who are open to belief, but never enough for those who are blind to their own need for redemption. And yet it is through the gospel message preached in the power of the Spirit that God saves those who believe.

The Cross, an Offense to Our Wisdom

While the Jews asked for a sign, the Greeks sought wisdom (1 Corinthians 1:22). Plato and Aristotle were among the most brilliant men who ever lived on planet earth. Their philosophies are still the stuff of doctoral dissertations and debate. Yet Plato wished that he had a "shaft of light" that would guide him in his quest to find the meaning of the world. There were other Greek philosophers who spent a lifetime seeking to probe the depths of ultimate questions. They sought the *summum bonum*—that is, the highest good.

To the Greeks God was *apatheia*—He was devoid of the ability to feel either pleasure or pain. He was both unconcerned and unaffected by our actions on earth. It was an insult to think He was involved in human affairs. Like people today, they believed in God, but not the right one.

When Paul stood on Mars Hill, he spoke to two different kinds of philosophers. Present were the Epicureans, the materialists of the day who believed that the world was made up only of atoms, and matter was the final reality. There was no soul, no immortality—there were no spirits in the world. All that existed was matter. They were the humanists of the day who would have agreed with the late Carl Sagan, who said, "The cosmos is all there is and all there ever will be."

The Epicureans were also hedonists; they believed that pleasure was the highest good. They did not believe in wanton pleasure, but argued that one should have a balance of pleasures. And yet the ultimate good was found in "feeling just right." Does that sound familiar?

Also present on Mars Hill were the Stoics, the pantheists. They were the New Agers of their day, believing that the final reality in the world was spirit. They believed in the immortality of the soul and the eventual absorption of the soul into the divine. They were into astrology and healing. They would have felt at home with the modern-day gurus who tout psychic realities, hypnosis, and a host of other New Age techniques. They also believed in virtue for its own sake; they believed that all should strive to be indifferent to good and evil, pleasure and pain. They adopted the fatalistic dictum, "Whatever will be, will be."

Both groups of philosophers agreed on this: If there was any salvation needed, it would come by ideas. Man's problem was not sin but ignorance. They were insulted by the thought that God would actually reveal Himself to the human race, and even more offended at the suggestion that God had to intervene in the human race to rescue people from sin. Such ideas were degrading to the human spirit and an affront to their gods.

But, after Paul preached to that crowd on Mars Hill, some of them became believers. Paul did not perform a miracle; nor did he try to answer all of the objections that swarmed into the Greek mind. "God was well-pleased through the foolishness of the message preached to save those who believe" (1 Corinthians 1:21). The news that we are not saved by our lifestyle but by the horrid death of another is initially repugnant to many people, but thankfully it is this message that has the power to overcome the natural resistance of the human will. And it is this message that we must proclaim anew in our day.

The Cross, an Offense to Our Values

The cross inverts our values. Like the prankster who switches the price tags of items in a store, the cross makes a mockery of the standards by which we judge ourselves and others. Paul wrote,

> Consider your calling, brethren, that there were not many wise according to the flesh, not many mighty, not many noble; but God has chosen the foolish things of the world to shame the wise, and God has chosen the weak things of the world to shame the things which are strong, and the base things of the world and the despised, God has chosen, the things that are not, that He might nullify the things that

are, that no man should boast before God (1 Corinthians 1:26-29).

God has taken those who are of no account in the world and elevated them to the status of sons and daughters. Those who are passed over by the standards of the world are singled out for special recognition. This offends people's sense of fairness.

In the first century of the church's existence, people from all walks of life came to faith in Christ. But the majority of the believers came from among the 60 million slaves of the Roman Empire. These were the lower class, the "living tools" as they were called. They had no discernible rights; they lived to do whatever the master wanted, and if the master wanted to murder them, he was free to do so.

Before the ages, God took some of those people and chose them to be heirs of His kingdom. "The base things of this world and the despised, God has chosen, the things that are not, that He might nullify the things that are, that no man should boast before God" (verses 28,29). The cross affirmed that at least some people who did not matter to men mattered to God. Queen Victoria, it is said, read this passage of Scripture and exclaimed, "Thank God for the letter *m!*" The reason is because in verse 26 we read, "Consider your calling, brethren, that there were not many wise according to the flesh, not many mighty, not many noble." The queen was grateful that the text did not say, "Not *any* mighty or *any* noble" were called. It simply said not *many!* And she was among the few.

The doctrine of the cross is troubling because of its exclusivity. Philosopher David Hume taught that it was immoral for God to limit salvation to a small group of people who lived at a particular time and in a particular location. "If God is going to save some he is under obligation to save all," the unconverted mind reasons. Thus the offense of the cross is magnified. And yet, in that offense is the "power of God for salvation." It is a message this generation has to hear.

The Cross and Society

The cross stands as a witness to the failure of men. In its presence the cult of self-expression lies in ruins. It runs counter to the inflated egoism that is seen on talk shows and in self-help books. When I asked a friend whether his cousin had been helped by seeing a counselor he responded, "They gave him so much self-esteem that no one could live with him!"

The Jews failed; the Greeks failed; we all have failed. We are not only failures, but we are also equal failures. We have all been included under sin that God might have mercy on those who believe, "for there is no distinction; for all have sinned and fall short of the glory of God" (Romans 3:22,23).

To accept the cross is to adopt an entirely different worldview. The woman who wore the cross of Christ on her necklace along with a trinket that symbolized the Hindu god Om will think differently once she is converted. I do not know if she will ever come to faith in Christ, but if she does it will be because God overcame the blindness of her heart through the offensive message of the cross.

It is easy for people to pray to Christ and even "receive Him" because He is a worthy teacher and mentor, or even because He is the Savior. But a faith that falls short of a miracle wrought by God cannot save. Luther, I believe, was right when he criticized the mystics of his day for wanting to crawl up to God and "see Him naked." It is people like them who try to ascend their own ladder to God and bypass the cross.

To accept the cross is to experience the power of God. Don't be discouraged because men and women by nature despise the cross. Once they have heard the message, lovingly given, they become intrigued by it. Perhaps they will reject it, but their curiosity might well continue. They become impressed by the life of the authentic Christian who proves, through acts of kindness, that the cross actually can change human nature.

The very message that the world despises is the message that it needs. We can make the message as understandable as possible, but we cannot avoid it. We are not in a cultural war, but a theological war. Now we can understand why Paul told the church at Corinth that he came with the singular motive of preaching the gospel: "I determined to know nothing among you except Jesus Christ, and Him crucified. And I was with you in weakness and fear and in much trembling" (1 Corinthians 2:2,3). Unlike some of us who often preach the gospel with a sense of propriety and haughty confidence, Paul was humbled, deliberately eschewing superiority of speech or wisdom. He knew that God alone does the saving.

How I wish that modern-day evangelists had the same fear Paul had. He feared that the faith of some of His listeners might rest in the wisdom of men rather than the power of God: "My message and my preaching were not in persuasive words of wisdom, but in demonstration of the Spirit and of power, that your faith should not rest on the wisdom of men, but on the power of God" (verses 4,5). He acknowledged the possibility that some people might think they had come to belief in Christ when in actuality they were responding to the message from a wrong motive and with a skewed understanding. Human wisdom is very capable of perverting the purity of the divine message.

Unfortunately, too few of us share the same fear Paul had. Often we couch the cross in sweet phrases, easy believism, and "decisional regeneration." We tell our listeners that eternal life is theirs to choose if only they will come forward in a meeting, pray a prayer, and sign a decision card. We are afraid to tell them how helpless they really are, and point out their desperate need to transfer all of their trust to Christ in repentance and faith. We all know about evangelistic campaigns where thousands were "converted" but a month later we can scarcely find a single convert.

Though we profess to believe in another world, it is easy for us to live as if this is the only one that really matters. It is easy for us to hide behind our creature comforts rather than carry our cross. How easy it is for us to forget that God's work must be done in God's way.

Accepting the Cross on God's Terms

Finally, the cross gives no glory to man, but always points to God. The reason for choosing those who are despised and often bypassing those who see themselves as belonging to the upper echelons of society is that "no man should boast before God" (1 Corinthians 1:29).

In *The Mustard Seed Conspiracy,* Tom Sine writes,

> Jesus let us in on an astonishing secret. God has chosen to change the world through the lowly, the unassuming, and the imperceptible. . . . That has always been God's strategy, changing the world though the conspiracy of the insignificant. He chose a ragged bunch of Semite slaves to become the insurgents of his new order. . . . And who would have ever dreamed that God would choose to work through a baby in a cow stall to turn the world right side up![1]

God gets the glory when a small group of Christians makes an impact in society that is much greater than their numbers. He is glorified when His people are gifted beyond their natural ability. And He is glorified when the cross is shared without shame and hesitancy.

Two thieves were crucified with Christ—one on His right, the other on His left. The one represented the sign-seekers: "Are You not the Christ? Save Yourself and us!" (Luke 23:39). The other looked at Christ, who appeared to be as helpless as he himself was, and cried, "Remember me when you come in Your kingdom!" (verse 42).

Think of the latter man's faith!

Upon the cross, Christ did not appear to be the son of God; He did not appear to be winning the battle against death. He was hanging there with blood running down his distraught body, with no evidence that He was qualified to win the war against death. And yet this thief, bless him, understood that in His weakness, the man writhing next to him was strong, *and in His death, there was eternal life.*

To him Christ replied, "Today you shall be with Me in Paradise."

Surely no words could be sweeter to a sinner who needed to be saved.

Henry Lyte spent the last 23 years of his life ministering to an Anglican parish in Devonshire, England. He humbly served the Lord in the midst of a difficult and hardened community. He did not see all the results he desired. Among his many hymns are these familiar words:

> *Jesus, I my cross have taken, All to leave and follow Thee*
> *Destitute, despised forsaken, Thou from hence my all shall be*
> *Perish every fond ambition, All I've sought and hoped and known*
> *Yet, how rich is my condition, God and heaven are still my own.*

If we had been in Christ's place, most likely we would have called 12 legions of angels to deliver us, and to do it fast. We simply do not want to be treated like our Master; we would rather sue our opponent if necessary to "defend our rights." Repeatedly we confront the world on its own terms and we lose. Let us never forget, then, that "the foolishness of God is wiser than men, and the weakness of God is stronger than men" (1 Corinthians 1:25).

We are sent as sheep among wolves ... but God's strength is made perfect in our weakness.

FIVE

The Cross, the Suffering of God

God cares about the world.

That statement lies at the heart of the Christian faith. But many unbelievers do not want to hear what we have to say because they believe that the God of Christianity is indifferent to the sufferings of this planet. They believe the gods of New Age religion, the gods of the east, are more compatible with our plight because these deities do not claim omnipotence. A god who resides within us can hardly be responsible for the evils of the world. But the Christian God—the Being who exists independently of the universe, a personal being who answers prayer and supposedly created the universe in the first place—such a being is more culpable. A God who sees human suffering and fails to intervene is hardly worthy of worship.

What do you say to a skeptic who reasons this way?

Perhaps you would be tempted to remind him of the sun and rain that cause crops to grow so that we can eat. The skeptic would be unconvinced; yes, there are rain showers but also floods, hurricanes, and tornadoes. In some places, the earth is firm, but in other countries there are frequent earthquakes. Millions of people enjoy healthy lives, but others die an early and painful death of cancer. Take a hard look at nature, and you would never guess that God really cares.

Or, you might be tempted to point the skeptic to mankind. We all know people who care about each other; this must mean that God cares about us. But for every person who is loving there is someone who is cruel; for every generous person there is one who is greedy. Just look at the headlines of today's paper to see what people do to one another. Scant proof that there is a God who genuinely cares about the world!

We cannot get a hearing from a cynical world unless we can show that God cares, and that because He cares, people matter. False religions proliferate because of cynicism—the conviction that the Christian God has proven to be indifferent to the world's plight. Even those who would like to believe conclude that God isn't benevolent, and sadly, it appears as if His followers aren't either. Many people find Christians to be judgmental, self-serving, and unwilling to be uprooted from their comfortable lifestyles.

C.S. Lewis wrote that he was often on the verge of deception: "Not that I am in much danger of ceasing to believe in God. The real danger is to believe such dreadful things about Him. The conclusion I dread is not 'So there is really no God after all,' but 'So this is what God is really like.' Deceive yourself no longer."[1]

Do we have some reason to not think some dreadful things about God? Can we say with integrity that God cares and therefore people matter?

Only at the cross do we see the love of God without ambiguity. Here is God's farthest reach, His most ambitious rescue effort. God personally came to our side of the chasm, willing to suffer for us and with us. At the cross His love burst upon the world with unmistakable clarity. Here at last we have found solid reasons to believe that there was a genuine meeting between God and man. Here is mercy, here is justice. And here is a God who suffers with us.

At the cross, cynicism ends.

Although only the Holy Spirit is able to convince men and women of their need for Christ, our responsibility is to clarify the meaning of the cross and answer, as best we can, the hard questions that a skeptical world hurls at us. And, we ourselves need answers lest we end up thinking dreadful thoughts about the Almighty. As always, we must return to the cross.

Seeing God Clearly in the Cross

In the cross we see both a loving God and a suffering God. Here we see a God who has Himself faced the cruel blows of what is popularly called fate. Here we meet a God who will astound us and captivate our hearts. The more clearly we see Him, the more intensely we will love Him.

"God was in Christ reconciling the world unto Himself" (2 Corinthians 5:19). In those nine words we have the essence of the gospel, the assurance that God has drawn near. He has built a bridge to us and paid the entire cost of its construction. And He walks arm-in-arm with us over the chasm, entering into our own suffering … and honoring us beyond our wildest dreams.

To better understand the suffering of God we need to take a journey that begins at a familiar stream but ends in the deep river of God's lovingkindness and personalized grace. If we stare at the cross intently we will find a God who not only judges but also grieves—a God who not only smites, but also heals.

Let's consider three common words that will guide us to some uncommon blessings: substitution, submission, and suffering.

The Self-Substitution of God

The idea of *substitution* is as old as Eden, where God killed animals so that Adam and Eve would have a covering for their nakedness. Those animals shed their blood for our first parents in order to picture the coming of a better sacrifice in the distant future. From then on, the phrase "in the place of" would become the essence of Old Testament theology.

When Abraham was prevented from sacrificing Isaac, he saw "a ram caught in the thicket by his horns" (Genesis 22:13). Thus providentially Abraham went and took the ram, and offered him up for a burnt offering "in the place of his son." The very word *sacrifice* implies substitution.

When the Israelites were about to leave Egypt, they were instructed to sprinkle the blood of a lamb on their doorposts so the angel of death would bypass them. Thus the lamb died "in the place of" the firstborn in every Israelite home. But these lambs were only symbolic; they were unable to permanently shield the Israelites from judgment or take away the sins of the nation.

The substitute offered as a sacrifice has to have a value sufficient to bear the penalty. When sin entered into the world, there was no sacrifice that could have met the qualifications to actually redeem humanity. No animal could have qualified; nor could a perfect human being meet the unspeakable demands of God. If the barrier of sin that existed between us and God was to be removed, God would have to remove it Himself. Thankfully He did just that.

The prophet Isaiah, writing as though He were sitting at the foot of the cross, described Christ's mission:

> Surely our griefs He Himself bore, and our sorrows He carried; yet we ourselves esteemed Him stricken, smitten of God, and afflicted. But He was pierced through for our transgressions, He was crushed for our iniquities; the chastening for our well-being fell upon Him, and by His scourging we are healed. All of us like sheep have gone astray, each of us has turned to his own way; but the LORD has caused the iniquity of us all to fall on Him (Isaiah 53:4-6).

God, in Christ, chose to bear the penalty that He Himself demanded. God became both our judge and our substitute. He both sentenced us to eternal condemnation and paid that price on our behalf. Charles Cranfield made this observation in his commentary on Romans:

> God, because in His mercy He willed to forgive sinful men, and, being truly merciful, willed to forgive them righteously, that is, without in any way condoning their sin, purposed to direct against His own very self in the person of His son the full weight of that righteous wrath which they deserved.[2]

Recently a mother threw herself over her two-year-old son to absorb the impact of a car that was out of control. She was killed, but her child lived. She became the substitute, preserving the physical life of the one she dearly loved. She literally died "in the place of" her son. God rescued us from a more terrifying fate of eternal moral and spiritual lostness. And He put Himself in harm's way to absorb the blow. Calvin wrote, "This is our acquittal: the guilt that held us liable for punishment has been transferred to the head of the son of God."[3] We read in 1 Peter 2:24, "He Himself bore our sins in His body on the cross."

Recently while on a plane I spoke to a woman who wondered how I could be so sure of my relationship with God. "Can you be sure that if this plane went down you'd go to heaven?" she probed. I answered "Yes, I can be sure"—because I am convinced that Christ's sacrifice is all that God will ever require of me to stand before Him. Because the sacrifice was fully accepted, I am fully acquitted.

> Jesus paid it all.
> All to Him I owe;
> Sin had left a crimson stain,
> He washed it white as snow.

"The essence of sin is man substituting himself for God, while the essence of salvation is God substituting himself for man."[4] We now move from the familiar to the less familiar. Now we must probe the mystery of the Trinity and the role of the suffering God.

The Submission of God

Speaking of Christ, the Suffering Servant, Isaiah wrote:

> He was oppressed and He was afflicted, yet He did not open His mouth; like a lamb that is led to slaughter, and like a sheep that is silent before its shearers, so He did not open His mouth (Isaiah 53:7).

Christ was likened to a lamb not because he was weak, but because He was submissive. He could have called upon angels to deliver Him, but He went to the cross voluntarily to die for us.

Here we must avoid an error that we make too easily. The impression can be given that a benevolent Christ persuaded a reluctant God to do something about the plight of humanity and

He reluctantly agreed. The Father then took His anger against humanity and directed it toward Christ.

This popular understanding of the cross is often supported by statements that Christ was "smitten of God, and afflicted" and again, "The LORD was pleased to crush Him, putting Him to grief" (verses 4, 10). The image of an angry God exacting every ounce of payment from a submissive Christ can distort our understanding of the Almighty. If not properly understood in context, we can end up thinking some dreadful things about God. We can end up perceiving the Son as lovingly willing, but the Father as reluctant and harsh.

Such an outlook flounders in the face of God's love. Indeed, the saving work of God *originated* in Him; it is because of the "tender mercy of our God" that Christ came (Luke 1:78). The most famous verse in the Bible teaches that "God so loved the world, that He gave His only begotten Son...." The Father initiated salvation because of His lovingkindness; the Father is a redeeming God.

The Father and the Son took the initiative together. John Stott wrote,

> We must not, then, speak of God punishing Jesus or of Jesus persuading God, for to do so is to set them over against each other as if they acted independently of each other or were even in conflict with each other.... The Father did not lay on the Son an ordeal He was reluctant to bear, nor did the Son extract from the Father a salvation He was reluctant to bestow.[5]

Stott is right to point out that the will of the Father and the will of the Son coincided in the perfect self-sacrifice of love. We must never set the Son and the Father over against each other. If the Father turned away from the Son at the cross, it is because they agreed that it must be so, given the means of redemption that was chosen.

Just as the Trinity was unified in its decision to create the world, the Godhead was similarly unified in the greater act of redemption. Although the incarnation invites us to separate the persons of the Godhead, it does not allow us to see them in conflict. "God was in Christ reconciling the world to Himself" (2 Corinthians 5:19). This does not mean that God is our servant or that His primary motive is our happiness; it means simply that given the ends He wanted to accomplish, He chose to accommodate Himself to our great need of redemption. He submitted Himself to our need.

Now we are ready to move further downstream and wade in the deep waters of contemplation, where we will try to understand our suffering God. We must tread carefully, keeping in mind that we are entering into the mystery of the incarnation and crucifixion. Our challenge will be to stay within the confines of God's revelation and yet be able to say without fear that *God* suffered on our behalf.

The Suffering of God

That Christ suffered on the cross is, of course, acknowledged by all. His grief in Gethsemane, His expressions of sorrow, and His cries from the cross all testify of His personal agony and pain. "Surely our griefs He Himself bore, and our sorrows He carried" (Isaiah 53:14).

But did He suffer only as man, or also as God? Was the whole Trinity emotionally involved in His agony? Or was the divine nature passive while the Father was accepting the payment that was being made on that dark day in Jerusalem?

Can God suffer? *Did* God suffer?

In the early centuries of the church, there was much discussion regarding the impassibility of God—that is, the doctrine that He is incapable of feeling pain. This doctrine teaches that He has no emotions that are affected by what happens on earth—not that He is removed from us or indifferent, but that He is unaffected by our trauma. It was widely taught that He stays above the fray, granting us His grace but not suffering with us in our pain. Because He is immutable, the Lord who changes not, emotional ups and downs would be inconsistent with His perfections.

The Westminster Confession of Faith asserts that God "is without body, parts, or passions, immutable." Even some contemporary theologians have argued that only the human nature of Christ suffered on the cross, not the divine. The love of Christ, they say, was the love of God, the power of Christ was the power of God, but the suffering of Christ did not belong to the Godhead. God could not suffer in the incarnation as the God-man. It was His humanity alone that heaved with emotion the night before His crucifixion.

Is this biblical?

Some theologians argue, perhaps correctly, that the idea of the impassibility of God was unduly influenced by Greek philosophy, which taught that the gods were above pleasure and pain. Yet we also know that it would be disrespectful to say that God is a victim of His emotions and like us cannot do much about His changing moods or feelings.

That said, we must say emphatically that God has emotions, and that on the cross God suffered. Dennis Ngien argues that a God who cannot suffer is a God who cannot love. If God does not feel the pain of His people, it would be difficult to refute the conclusion that He is indifferent to our plight. "God suffers" says Ngien, "because He wills to love."[6] Dietrich Bonhoeffer was right when he wrote from prison, "Only a suffering God can help." Suffering is not a sign of weakness, but entails a decision to love.

If only the humanity of Christ suffered at the cross, then there was no real incarnation. Indeed, it might lead to the conclusion that only a man died on the cross, not the God-man. John Austin Baker correctly observed, "The crucified Jesus is the only accurate picture of God the world has ever seen."

Certainly the Bible is filled with references about God's emotion, such as His anger or His compassion. Read these texts and sense the pathos of God:

> "Is Ephraim My dear son? Is he a delightful child? Indeed, as often as I have spoken against him, I certainly still remember him; therefore My heart yearns for him; I will surely have mercy on him," declares the LORD (Jeremiah 31:20).

> Can a woman forget her nursing child, and have no compassion on the son of her womb? Even these may forget, but I will not forget you (Isaiah 49:15).

> How can I give you up, O Ephraim? How can I surrender you, O Israel? How can I make you like Admah? How can I treat you like Zeboiim? My heart is turned over within Me, all My compassions are kindled. I will not execute My fierce anger; I will not destroy Ephraim again. For I am God and not man, the Holy One in your midst, and I will not come in wrath (Hosea 11:8-9).

In those passages we see both the passionate love of God and burning wrath of God vividly described. Since we are made in the image of God, it must be that God has emotions. Certainly if the Holy Spirit is grieved because of our sin, we can say the same of the Father.

Is this contrary to the immutability of God? Does it imply that God is frustrated, like a jilted lover who wishes he could make his dearest love him but is incapable of doing so?

Not at all. Bear in mind that *God chose to suffer.* He has chosen to be rejected by some and accepted by others. He suffered because He willed it so; as far as we know, He could have willed otherwise. He had before Him an indefinite number of possible worlds—worlds in which there was no fall, no sin, no need for redemption. Yet He chose this plan with its injustice and pain. We are invited to believe that, looked at from eternity, this plan is best.

By contrast, we suffer involuntarily. The circumstances of life with their mixture of joys and sorrows are largely out of our hands. But everything is in God's hands—*everything.* He suffers because He chooses to. No man can make God suffer. Someone once said that "He suffers by divine consent."

Let us say boldly that when you see Christ on the cross, you see God. There is no inconsistency between the suffering of the Messiah and the nature of God. Christ said pointedly, "He who has seen me has seen the Father" (John 14:9). It simply is not possible to separate Christ as man from Christ as God. The suffering of Christ is really God's own suffering. "God, dying for man," wrote P.T. Forsyth. "I am not afraid of that phrase; I cannot do without it. God dying for men; and for such men—hostile, malignantly hostile men." He went on to say, "God must either inflict punishment or assume it. And He chose the latter course, as honoring the law while saving the guilty. He took His own judgment."[7]

Bishop Stephen Neill wrote, "If the crucifixion of Jesus ... is in some way, as Christians have believed, the dying of God himself, then ... we can understand what God is like."[8] Yet the Scriptures do stop short of saying, "God died...." The reason is because immortality belongs to God's essential being, "who alone possesses immortality and dwells in unapproachable light; whom no man has seen or can see. To Him be honor and eternal dominion! Amen" (1 Timothy 6:16). So He became a *man* that He might be able to die.

Perhaps Paul's admonition to the Ephesian elders is the closest the Scriptures come to saying that God died. He said, "Be on guard for yourselves and for all the flock, among which the Holy Spirit has made you overseers, to shepherd the church of God which He purchased with His own blood" (Acts 20:28). The church, he said, was purchased by the blood of God!

Perhaps a second reason why the Bible does not say explicitly that God died is because God, in the New Testament, is frequently called "Father." And the person who died on the cross was not the Father, but the Son. Yet we must remember that the two persons of the Godhead cannot be separated. "All these things are from God, who reconciled us to Himself through Christ, and gave us the ministry of reconciliation" (2 Corinthians 5:17-18). Stott again urges us to remain balanced: "If we speak only of Christ suffering and dying, we overlook the initiative of the Father. If we speak only of God suffering and dying, we overlook the mediation of the Son.... God [was] acting in and through Christ with His whole-hearted concurrence."[9]

George Butterick describes for us a picture of the crucifixion in an Italian church. In the picture is a vast and shadowy figure behind the portrait of Christ. The nail that pierces the hand of Jesus goes through to the hand of God. The spear thrust into the side of Jesus goes through into God's.[10] Luther said that if it is not true that God died for us, but only a man died, then we are lost.

It is unthinkable that Christ would cry, "My God, My God, why hast Thou forsaken Me?" and the Father not suffer. As parents, we know that if we watched our son die he would not be the only one suffering. With that in mind, think of the even closer relationship that exists between the members of the Trinity! Indeed, they are one in essence, one in purpose, and one in desire. If Christ suffered as man, we must boldly affirm that God suffered also.

A Word for Our Suffering World

Phil Donahue, a former talk-show host, once listed the various reasons why he became disillusioned with Christianity. Among them was this: "How could an all-knowing, all-loving God allow His Son to be murdered on a cross in order to redeem my sins? If God the Father is so 'all loving,' why didn't *He* come down and go to Calvary?" The answer is, "In Christ, *He did!*"

The little girl who says, "I love Jesus, but I am afraid of God" needs to have her theology corrected. If Jesus cares about her—and He does—God cares about her, too. And if Christ is touched with her pain, God is touched with her pain as well. Let us remember that His heart cannot be separated from that of His Son. "Hear O Israel! The LORD is our God, the LORD is One!" Let us not think wrong things about God.

Is God compassionate? Does He feel the pain of His creation? I believe the answer is *yes*. "There is only one means to endure our suffering, and that is to understand His, to hook ours onto His, and to remember that ours is His," writes Louis Evely. Recall the woman whose son was killed in an accident—in anger she asked her pastor, "Where was your God when my son was killed?" The pastor replied, "He was in the same place where He was when His Son was killed."

Our perpetual struggle is to reconcile God's love and the fact of human suffering. We may sometimes feel as if God has turned on us in our greatest hour of need. What we want in our despair is an unveiling of God's heart—we want to know that He not only has power, but that He also has feelings. We all have seen the pain on the face of a child when a parent remains aloof from his suffering. We can be glad that our heavenly Father is not like that; He not only knows, He feels.

If it was God in Christ who was murdered on the cross—if it was God who willingly allowed the forces of evil to close in on Him—then we have just uncovered another way in which Christianity differs from all other religions. Christianity says that God willingly accepted mistreatment at the hands of His creatures. We have a God with loving wounds.

God's suffering, I believe, did not end with the cross. He continues to suffer with us in our fallenness. God does not delight in seeing us suffer, but He has hidden purposes to which He is directing all things. "When you pass through the waters, I will be with you; and through the rivers, they will not overflow you. When you walk through the fire, you will not be scorched, nor will the flame burn you. For I am the LORD your God, The Holy One of Israel, your Savior" (Isaiah 43:2,3). The sorrows of earth are felt in heaven.

We must not paint the picture of man's affliction as observed by a distant and only occasionally caring God. God feels our pains and hurts; Christ is "touched with the feeling of our infirmities" (Hebrews 4:15 KJV). To the young man who was a disciple of Christ but left the faith after his sister was brutally murdered I say, "God cares and feels!" God is not calloused because He has observed so much evil from the time of the Fall. He has not been desensitized by the centuries of violence and pain.

To the woman who lives with an angry, uncaring husband I can say with integrity, "God suffers with you." God loves us with an everlasting love. If the word *love* has any meaning at all, it must mean that God feels our heartaches. "Just as a father has compassion on his children, so the LORD has compassion on those who fear Him. For He Himself knows our frame; He is mindful that we are but dust" (Psalm 103:13,14).

God is the silent sufferer; He knows, understands, and cares. He carries our sorrows close to His heart. When Christ asked Saul, who persecuted Christians, "Saul, why do you persecute me?" He was implying that He himself felt the blows and the pangs of injustice. And since God is one, the Father felt those blows, too.

This does not mean that we have answered all of our questions about God and suffering. But that we can say that God loves us—the cross is evidence of that. Also, since God *chose* to suffer, it must be for a grand purpose, no matter how hidden it might be to us. Our comfort lies in the fact that our God not only walks with us, but feels with us in our sorrows and distresses. And someday, we will more fully understand.

Our Call to Suffer

Bonhoeffer said accurately that "suffering is not an interruption, but our calling." Paul wrote that we are to share in the sufferings of Christ. This is the pain we endure because of Christ, the choice we make because He is our example. In our suffering we become conformed to His likeness.

As our culture drifts further into paganism, we as Christians fear the suffering that might come our way. Employees fear that they might not be able to witness for Christ given new laws that declare that workplaces are "religion free." Parents feel increasingly intimidated or silenced by the school systems that promote homosexual lifestyles, sexual freedom, and radical individualism. Churches fear they will lose their tax-exempt status if they do not marry homosexual couples.

Dire suffering—indeed, *any* suffering for Christ in our culture—is largely unknown to us. But other countries have not been exempt; in fact, there are more people dying for their faith today in the face of hostile cultures and political regimes than at any other time in history. Perhaps that kind of suffering will come our way soon.

To quote Bonhoeffer once more:

> Where the world exploits [the Christian] will dispossess himself, and where the world oppresses, he will stoop down and raise up the oppressed. If the world refuses justice, the Christian will pursue mercy, and if the world takes refuge in lies, he will open his mouth for the dumb, and bear testimony to the truth.... for Jew or Greek, bond or free, strong or weak, noble or base.[11]

Peter wrote, "You have been called for this purpose, since Christ also suffered for you leaving you an example for you to follow in His steps" (1 Peter 2:21). And again, "Beloved, do not be surprised at the fiery ordeal among you, which comes upon you for your testing, as though some strange thing were happening to you; but to the degree that you share the sufferings of Christ, keep on rejoicing; so that also at the revelation of His glory, you may rejoice with exultation" (4:12,13). It is not how loud we can shout but how well we can suffer that will convince the world of the integrity of our message.

Michael Baumgarten, a nineteenth-century Lutheran pastor who was excommunicated because of his adherence to a true gospel, wrote, "There are times in which lectures and publications no longer suffice to communicate the necessary truth. At such times the deeds and sufferings of the saints must create a new alphabet in order to reveal again the secret of truth."[12] Suffering communicates the gospel in a new language; it authenticates the syllables that flow so easily from our lips. When the chaff is separated from the wheat, the kernels germinate and grow.

Yet should we not do everything possible to maintain our freedoms? Certainly, for we are invited to do that in a democracy. The old adage that we should change what we can, accept what we can't, and pray that we will know the difference is always relevant. However, when we do not win our "cultural wars," we must willingly suffer like Christ. How can we participate in His suffering if we refuse to forgive those who have wronged us, believing that God will eventually set the record straight? Will not our witness be compromised if we continue to insist on our rights and adopt a victim mentality? Is not our future on earth in the hands of our heavenly Father, who knows, cares, and feels?

A missionary to Kenya, after describing the fiery ordeals of Christian converts there, including mutilation and death by terrorists, said this about the converts, "I am constantly humbled by their patience and lack of bitterness, which springs from an acceptance of the cross in their lives."[13] Like the early church, we represent Christ best when we rejoice that we are "considered worthy to suffer shame for His name" (Acts 5:41).

Helmut Thielicke was asked his assessment of American Christians, and he replied that they have an inadequate view of suffering. "The average American" he said, "believes that suffering is something fundamentally inadmissible." We might add "and unconstitutional." Many of us simply are not ready to suffer for the sake of the gospel. Many believing college students are not ready to jeopardize their degree by countering so-called politically correct thought at their university, even if the matter concerns the sharing of the gospel. Christian employees often allow themselves to be silenced by laws against religious expression, and Christian nurses sometimes participate in abortions to keep their jobs.

Amazing Love

Christ endured the cross for "the joy set before Him" (Hebrews 12:2). He knew that suffering preceded glory; the cross came before the crown. In the same way we must have the faith to believe that God will walk with us through whatever trials He might expect us to endure. What is more, these trials are intended to increase our eternal joy and happiness. No suffering is wasted; no opportunity to share in His trials should be bypassed: "... and if children, heirs also, heirs of God and fellow heirs with Christ, if indeed we suffer with Him in order that we may also be glorified with Him" (Romans 8:17).

In Colossians 1:24 Paul wrote, "I rejoice in my sufferings for your sake, and in my flesh I do my share on behalf of His body (which is the church) in filling up that which is lacking in Christ's afflictions." The cross we take into the world proclaims this message to a cynical generation: God cares; indeed, God has chosen to feel the pain of His creation. He does not stand aloof; having personally shared in our grief, He stands by to help us, love us, and eventually take us to be with Himself.

We cannot say that we have solved the mystery of suffering. Yet we can endure suffering much better when we know that the Trinity is for us—a Trinity that has personally tasted the grief that confronts us in a sinful world. Charles Wesley did not back away from the bold assertion:

> *Amazing love! How can it be*
> *That Thou, my God, shouldst die for me?*

The Cross of Reconciliation

Today our culture is fragmenting.

The founding fathers believed that America was to be a melting pot—that the diverse ethnic and racial groups would retain their identity, but be united with one constitution, "one nation under God."

John Quincy Adams wrote that immigrants must "cast off their European skin, never to resume it; they must look forward to their posterity rather than backward to their ancestors." He would, I believe, have been opposed to our present-day cult of "ethnicity," which insists that every group should be identified with their past rather than become part of the American melting pot. Today we have African Americans, Asian Americans, Hispanic Americans, Anglo Americans, and a host of other groups who want to be identified by their past roots rather than their present status as citizens. Far from coming together, we seem to be drifting further apart.

The O.J. Simpson trial reminded Americans that racial animosity lies close to the surface, held in check with civility but ready to explode when provoked. Blacks accused whites of assuming Simpson was guilty simply because he was black; whites accused blacks of wanting him acquitted simply because he was a member of their tribe. Despite the gains that have been made in the civil rights movement, it is difficult to uproot racism from the human heart.

We are also divided economically. We have the rich and the poor, the servants and the masters, the suburbs and the inner cities. Unfortunately poverty continues to increase, resistant to government cures. Despite massive amounts of money for welfare, Medicaid, and subsidized work programs, many are still poor and angry about it. And with cuts in welfare, for some people the situation is bleak indeed.

We are divided religiously; we have Protestants, Catholics, Muslims, Hindus, Buddhists, and other religious groups adapting to American culture and competing for the minds and hearts of our population. A Muslim flight attendant complained that her airline was violating her religious beliefs by prohibiting her from wearing a *hijab*, or head scarf. The U.S. Equal Employment Opportunity Commission agreed, and sued the airline for discrimination. With a number of different religious groups demanding their "rights," we are indeed a nation where the notion of equality is being tested.

We are also divided domestically—that is, family life is disintegrating. The high divorce rate, the escalation of abuse, and the increasing number of latchkey children all testify to the emotional deprivation of this generation. We are living together in a nation that is disconnected, unable to form deep and lasting relationships. George Barna describes us as "a fast-paced, experience-driven, multiple-option world, where personal values pale beside the possibility of exposure to the latest, the biggest, the fastest, the most prestigious, the best, or the most expensive."

The Barriers to Reconciliation

In such a world, many relationships are either brief, high-intensity encounters which quickly burn themselves out, or casual interactions that do not fill the human desire for love and a lasting connection. Americans are, for the most part, a lonely lot, seeking to fill the void with the latest gadgets or entertainment venues. Deep relationships characterized by loyalty and commitment are few in number and little is done to encourage them. Thus our desires are unmet, and as a nation we keep turning to those solutions that only inflame greater unmet desires.

To where do we turn?

The church is called to model wholesome, caring relationships in a culture that no longer believes that such friendships are possible. Our calling is to eschew that part of our culture that is fueled by a radical individualism that selfishly seeks one's own "good" at the expense of one's neighbor. We have to prove that deep and loyal friendships can exist among those who otherwise have racial, cultural, and economic differences. In other words, we are to model the oneness for which Christ prayed. It is at this very point that we should be most unlike the world.

Sin always divides. When Adam and Eve disobeyed, they were separated from God and their children were separated from one another. Cain killed Abel, and from that time onward the history of the human race has been marked by fragmentation and broken relationships. When man tried to remain unified by building the tower of Babel, God judged the human race because it strove for unity amid idolatry and personal self-interest.

And today, sin continues to divide us. Here are some musings that reflect well the attitudes that prevail in our world today:

> *My pride means that I am better than you and cannot accept you unless you are on my level. You must conform to my standards of hygiene, diet, and work ethic. If not, I will deem you inferior. No matter how kind I appear to you on the outside, within my heart you are despised.*

> *My greed means that you cannot touch what is mine. I have worked for it. And if you do not have the same amount of money I have, you are lazy and mentally challenged. You had better not take what belongs to me because I will fight for what is mine—no matter how great your need. After all, that is just the American way.*

> *If you appeal to me—if I like your personality and your appearance and you make me feel good about myself—I will like you. If you begin to drain my emotional energy without making me feel appreciated, I will drop the relationship, the sooner the better. I need relationships that meet my needs, not relationships where I meet the needs of someone else.*

The reason we might not even be aware of these attitudes that lie like a coiled serpent in the bottom of our hearts is because America is a large country that offers us almost unlimited options. We can live where we like, chose whatever vocation we want, and move from one part of the country to another as it strikes our fancy. This means that we can avoid living and working with those who are different from us. Our prejudices can remain unchallenged.

When my wife and I visited Russia we learned that because of a severe housing shortage, it is common for two families to live in one small apartment. Most of us probably can't imagine what it would be like to share the same kitchen, living room, and closets with another family. That certainly would be a challenge to our well-polished persona. In such close quarters, the true nature of our hearts would be revealed. I'm sure that we would be surprised at our own selfishness, anger, and impatience. Friends we love dearly might be despised in a close environment where petty jealousies and favoritism have the opportunity to surface daily.

Thankfully, we do not have to live in such conditions in America. But at the same time, it is because of our unlimited options that we have not had to face up to our own prejudices and selfishness. We say, "As long as you stay in your corner and I stay in mine, we should be able to get along fine, thank you. And if not, I will move!"

God expects more than that. He wants us to be united within our *hearts*. Biblical unity is not simply peaceful co-existence. It means that I am willing to subject my own personal interests for your good; it means that I can demonstrate love for those whom I by nature would despise. It means that I am willing to put my life on the line for someone else. It means nothing less than the love of a crucified Savior living in my heart. This is the cross that we are commanded to take into the world.

Think of the hostility that presently exists between the Jews and the Arabs. This centuries-old conflict is so deeply rooted in the hearts of those who share the land of Israel that the rules of rationality simply do not apply. A peace treaty might be honored out of political necessity, but it will not be honored out of love. No piece of paper can change the human heart. And no reasons are compelling enough to cease the animosity.

This same hatred existed between many of the Jews and Gentiles in the first century A.D. The Jews, because they were God's chosen people, thought they were better than others. They forgot that God chose them even though they were stiff-necked and otherwise quite unattractive (Exodus 32:9). We've already learned that God usually chooses those who are on the lower rung of the ladder rather than those who are at the top. To be chosen of God should have spawned humility, not pride.

In that era, if a Jewish man or woman married a Gentile, a funeral was held for that man or woman. Even to help a Gentile mother give birth was forbidden, since this would be helping another Gentile to be born into the world. To go to a Gentile house would render a Jew unclean. The Jews withheld the message of reconciliation from the Gentiles and then cursed them for not being chosen! In fact, they said that the Gentiles were created to fuel the fires of hell.

At the temple there was a series of courtyards, each a little higher than the one before. The court of the Gentiles was the farthest from the temple area, with a wall separating it from the inner courts. A sign on the wall read, "No foreigner may enter within the barricade which surrounds the sanctuary and enclosure." For a Gentile to enter meant death.

The Jews and Gentiles were not just separated religiously, but also racially. When Christ spoke to the Samaritan woman at Jacob's well, he broke two taboos simultaneously. In Jewish culture, men never spoke to an unknown woman with respect. Also Christ was speaking to someone who was racially mixed; she was part Assyrian, which was unforgivable. The Jews were proud that Abraham was their father, and in their mind, a person with both Gentile and Jewish blood was more contemptible than a total pagan.

Finally, they were separated culturally. The Jews developed their art and symbolism from God's revelation, whereas the Gentiles (such as the Greeks) developed a civilization based on nature and human wisdom. The Jews despised pagan representations and, of course, the Gentiles despised the narrow-minded religious fervor of the Jews.

In ancient Jewish culture, women were routinely mistreated. They were barred from the inner sanctuary of the temple area, and were seen as living to serve men. Each day Jewish men prayed, "O God, I thank Thee that I am not a woman." A Jewish man could divorce his wife for no reason at all and send her away without any due consideration. It was definitely a man's world—a *cruel* man's world.

The cross changed all this.

Let the Walls Fall Down

Christ came to demolish the barriers that existed between the Jews and Gentiles. Paul wrote that Christ "broke down the barrier of the dividing wall, by abolishing in His flesh the enmity, which is the Law of commandments contained in ordinances, that in Himself He might make the two into one new man, thus establishing peace" (Ephesians 2:14,15).

Christ demolished the wall (best represented by the law) between these two groups. The many numerous regulations of the Old Testament, including the dietary requirements and priestly functions, stood as a barrier between Jews and Gentiles. Christ did away with all that, having Himself become "the end of the law ... to everyone who believes" (Romans 10:4). The distinctions that God had made between Jew and Gentile no longer applied.

The sign that forbade the Gentiles to enter into the inner court of the sanctuary had to be set aside—for all. To dramatize the new era, the veil in the temple's Holy of Holies was split from top to bottom when Christ died. The cross opened the way for everyone to come to God though the blood that was shed. In the Old Testament God Himself had told the people to keep their distance from His presence, which was localized in the Holy of Holies. Now the new message was, "Come! Come on the basis of the cross, and come from all corners of the earth!"

The Jews and Gentiles were made one in Christ. For those who accept the Messiah "there is neither Jew nor Greek, there is neither slave nor free man, there is neither male nor female; for you are all one in Christ Jesus. And if you belong to Christ, then you are Abraham's offspring, heirs according to promise" (Galatians 3:28,29).

Four times in Ephesians 2 Paul uses the three-letter word "one" to describe the unity between Jew and Gentile. Christ "made both groups into *one*" (verse 14); He made "the two into *one* new man, thus establishing peace" (verse 15); He reconciled them "both in *one* body to God through the cross, having put to death the enmity" (verse 16). And, "through Him we both have our access in *one* Spirit to the Father" (verse 18).

God always wounds only that He might heal; He destroys only that He might build. His desire was to create something entirely different: a true unity between Jew and Gentile that would be stronger than anything that might divide them. This was a peace treaty that actually changed the hearts of the parties who accepted it. This was a kind of unity that demonstrated the power of God, a unity that was beyond human power and analysis.

The Cross, a New Creation

Paul used three figures of speech to help us understand what God did through the cross.

A New Body

First, at the cross God created *a new body*. We are told that Jesus reconciled them "both in one body to God" (Ephesians 2:16). In 1 Corinthians chapter 12 Paul develops the imagery of the body, affirming both diversity and interdependence.

How did this unity come about? By the power of the Holy Spirit: "through Him we both have our access in one Spirit to the Father" (Ephesians 2:18). God does not have one Holy Spirit for African Americans, another for Asian Americans, and another for Anglo Americans. We are all indwelt by the same Holy Spirit and have all been baptized into the same body. This is a genuine unity because we all share the same life. And we are responsive to Christ, the one head. It's a unity of accomplishment, where deeds are done together; therefore, sorrows and triumphs are shared.

A New Nation

Second, God created *a new nation:* "You are no longer strangers and aliens, but you are fellowcitizens with the saints, and are of God's household" (Ephesians 2:19). The church is a new nation, not marked by ethnicity.

The entire human race descended from the three sons of Noah: Shem, Ham, and Japheth. Thanks to the cross, descendants from all three sons became converted. Paul the apostle, a Shemite, was converted en route to Damascus by a special revelation of Christ. The Ethiopian treasurer, a descendent of Ham, was converted through the witness of Philip as he was returning home from a visit to Jerusalem. And Cornelius, a descendent of Japheth, was added to the body of Christ when Peter was finally willing to give up his prejudices and enter into the house of a Gentile.

What matters now is not a person's physical lineage, nor is it a matter of blood, for God has made "from one [blood], every nation of mankind to live on all the face of the earth, having determined their appointed times, and the boundaries of their habitation" (Acts 17:26). Medical professionals tell us that blood can be transfused across racial lines—it is a major common element we all share. So ancestry is not what determines our worth as individuals; on this we are all equal.

The unity of believers is now based on the fact that we have been begotten by the same Father in heaven. Christ is our brother, and the Holy Spirit is our companion. And this unity takes precedence over all racial histories. We are, says Paul, members of "the household of God."

Thus the cross speaks to our fragmented society, our disintegrating families. Those who were reared without acceptance and relationships should find their identity through the church. This is where the weak should be protected, the poor should be helped, and the lonely should find friends. This is where there can be genuine unity borne of love for the same Lord and for one another. In the face of our fragmenting families, we can belong to another family that will meet our needs for acceptance and love.

Christ invites us to His table as brothers and sisters. When Mary and Christ's half-brothers were finding it difficult to get close enough to speak to Him on account of a large crowd, Jesus said, "Who are My mother and My brothers?" Looking at those who were sitting around Him, He said, "Behold, My mother and My brothers! For whoever does the will of God, he is My brother and sister and mother" (Mark 3:33-35). Clearly, Jesus was saying that spiritual ties took precedence over blood ties. There is a body of unity more powerful than that of the human family: It is the family of God.

Bear in mind that Christ never prayed that the *world* would become one. We know that people in the world can unite for various causes: peace, the environment, lower taxes. These coalitions serve their purpose, but when individual interests collide with the cause, the members of the group leave and the group begins to dissolve. That's because these groups are collections of individuals that become united for a common goal. It is the agenda that brings a group together, and any disagreement over that agenda will spur disunity.

The church is much more than a group of individuals coming together under a common banner. It is more than a union based upon common interests and aspirations. We are not unified merely because we all have the same Holy Spirit indwelling us. The Scriptures teach that we actually become one metaphysically, spiritually, and internally. The interrelationship is so direct that if one part of the body suffers, the other parts will suffer with it.

Or, to say it differently, when we are divided by racism, personality conflicts, and egotistical turfism, we not only look bad but also the power of God in our lives is diminished. We are tearing at the very fabric of the unity for which Christ prayed. This is a unity in which we esteem others better than ourselves. When we become divisive, we grieve the Holy Spirit, who disregarded our differences when He saved us.

Spencer Perkins reminds us that there is a difference between *integration* and *reconciliation*. *Integration* is a political concept, *reconciliation* is spiritual. Integration forced some people to change their behavior. Reconciliation invites a change of heart. We may all agree that we need more laws that will force a change in behavior, but the even greater need is for a spiritual power that will change the attitude of the heart.

Perkins talks about the differences he and a white ministry partner had—they were so severe that even though the two intended to model reconciliation, they were thinking of separating, citing "irreconcilable differences." But they decided that they would go for counseling one last time to demonstrate that

they were "good Christians." He writes, "Neither of us was pre-
pared for the overwhelming simplicity, the complete absurdity,
and the illogical genius of God's amazing grace." He says that
although he knew the meaning of grace from his youth up, he
never thought of grace as a way of life. He continues, "I knew that
we are supposed to love one another as Christ loved us. But
somehow it was much easier for me to swallow the lofty untested
notion of dying for each other than simply giving grace to brothers
and sisters on a daily basis the way God gives us grace. Maybe I
was dense, but I just never got it." Only by giving one another grace
was reconciliation possible. They could either hold to their griev-
ances and insist that their hurts be redressed, or they could "trust
God when we lacked the ability to forgive. We chose grace."[1]

The cross means that we choose grace. Amid the petty judg-
ments of men, amid our many deeply held differences, we must
chose to forgive even when the forgiveness is not requested. Christ
on the cross said, "Father forgive them, for they know not what
they do." As Philip Yancey says, "Grace is unfair, which is one of the
hardest things about it. It is unreasonable to expect a woman to forgive the terrible things her father did to her, just because he apol-
ogizes many years later.... Grace, however, is not about fairness."[2]

A New Temple

We are also a *new temple*, built upon the foundation of the
apostles and prophets, Christ Jesus Himself being the cornerstone,
"in whom the whole building, being fitted together is growing into
a holy temple in the Lord; in whom you also are being built
together into a dwelling of God in the Spirit" (Ephesians 2:20-22).

During the days of Solomon, the workmen building the
temple went to a quarry and hewed stones that were perfectly
shaped for one another. When the stones were brought to

Jerusalem, they were mounted without the sound of a hammer or an axe. Similarly, God Himself goes into the quarry of sin and chooses stones to be used for building His temple. He is the architect, fitting the stones into the structure as He sees fit. The purpose of the new temple is not that we might enjoy the music that accompanies our services nor come to listen to sermons. These merely point to the greater purpose of God—namely, that we might be "built together into a dwelling of God in the Spirit." God is building a place where He can dwell.

When unbelievers are introduced to the church, they should say, "Surely God dwells among these people!" Paul says that the church should have the gift of prophecy so that if an unbeliever enters, "he is convicted by all, he is called to account by all; the secrets of his heart are disclosed; and so he will fall on his face and worship God, declaring that God is certainly among you" (1 Corinthians 14:24,25).

The cloud of glory that descended into the Holy of Holies during the time of Solomon departed a long time ago. God now resides among His people. When we are gathered in His name to worship, praise, and repent, God is most clearly seen. His agenda is to build a temple of redeemed people where His dwelling can become most evident. This cannot happen unless the stones are unified into a coherent whole, willing to be placed wherever the chief architect desires.

The High Cost of Reconciliation

If the cross is the high price Christ paid to bring unity between the Jews and Gentiles, then we cannot expect that our earthly expression of heavenly unity will be easily achieved. We need to be willing to forgive one another, humble ourselves before the Lord, and stand on common ground before Him.

When many caucasian Christians left the inner cities during the sixties and seventies on account of declining property values, they were conceding to the city of man rather than upholding the values of the city of God. Many of our inner cities were left with a great spiritual vacuum as churches that God had planted in our great population centers moved out to the suburbs. This migration to the suburbs proved that we are not willing to pay the price of a pilgrim but will run when our nest is disturbed.

We, as members of the church, must be willing to break out of our comfort zones and become meaningfully involved in the lives of people who are culturally, racially, and economically different from us. Our commitments must go beyond the superficial. We must be convinced that that which unites us is far stronger than that which can ever divide us.

God reconciles us to Himself, and then to each other. If I am reconciled to God and content with His grace, I need no longer be imprisoned in my narrow world. The protective shell that once said, "I cannot let you into my heart because it is already filled with myself" now has room for someone else. In fact, there is room for a lot of other people who don't even have to have anything in common with me.

What is the goal to which God is moving? He desires to redeem a transnational community of people who are as diverse as our cosmopolitan cities. If we would stand back and see the bigger picture, we would see multitudes of dots moving toward the mountain of God. Upon looking more closely, we would see that these dots are countless human beings—people from every tribe, tongue, and nation gathering to sing praises to the Lamb (see Revelation 7:9). Worthy is the Lamb!

God's purpose is so much larger than the United States—so much larger than the western world. God's purpose is to honor Himself by redeeming people from all the diverse tribes of the world. In that company of redeemed people, the racial *distinctions* will be maintained as proof that God's worldwide purpose was accomplished. But the *divisions* between the races—the prejudice and mistrust—will be gone forever. Gone too will be any feeling of superiority and the belief that some are entitled to a better existence than others because they were born into the right families.

If you are absolutely determined that you will never live in an interracial neighborhood, and your friends are limited to those who have the same skin color and background as you, I must warn you about heaven! God's redeemed community will reflect the diversity of race; it will show that He honors those who are of "mixed blood." *Anyone* who calls upon the name of the Lord will be saved, and our churches today should reflect this agenda.

Moving the Fence

During World War I some French soldiers brought the body of a comrade to a cemetery for burial. The priest told them gently that the cemetery was for Roman Catholics and he needed to ask whether the victim was a Catholic. They answered no, he was not. The priest said if that was the case, he could not permit burial in the churchyard. So the soldiers sadly took the body of their friend and buried him just outside the fence of the cemetery.

The next day they returned to mark the grave, but to their astonishment, they couldn't find it. They knew that they had buried him just next to the fence, but the freshly dug soil was not there. As they were about to leave, the priest saw them and told them what had happened. He said that his conscience had so troubled him that early in the morning, he had the fence moved outward to include the new grave within the parameters of the churchyard.

There is little chance that the world will be convinced that God dwells among us unless we are willing to move the fences. Not the doctrinal fences that define our faith (indeed, removing such fences is our most serious problem), but those cultural and personal fences that keep the body of Christ divided.

Some of us must move the fence of racism, admitting our prejudice and prideful hearts. Some of us need to move the fence of economics, becoming involved in helping the poor rather than being critical of them. Others need to move the barrier of personality or education. We must demonstrate that the unity we have in Christ is much greater than anything that could possibly divide us.

We must all find believers who are different from us and learn to love them for the sake of our mutual love for Jesus Christ. We must be willing to put to death the selfishness that keeps us in our own little circles, unwilling to win the goodwill and trust of our brothers and sisters. Edwin Markham wrote:

> *He drew a circle that shut me out—*
> *Heretic, rebel, a thing to flout.*
> *But Love and I had the wit to win:*
> *We drew a circle that took him in!*

As a church we have the responsibility of sharing the good news of Christ with people who are our friends but not yet our brothers and sisters. They are our neighbors but cannot yet be our prayer partners. We must widen our circles so that through us Christ is represented. Christ can bring together people who have been torn apart by sin. And this unity is a bridge to the world, proof that God exchanges animosity for love and acceptance for prejudice.

How does the cross bring about unity? Before the cross: 1) we are equally sinners. Here judgmentalism must come to its logical end. And 2) before the cross, we are equally accepted; God sees all believers as in Christ. Finally, 3) it is at the cross that we are all equally blessed. We stand as those who have inherited a mighty kingdom through the gracious providence of our God.

The early church was a society of love and mutual care which astonished the pagans and was recognized as something entirely new. It lent credibility to the claim that the new age had dawned in Christ. The word was not only announced but seen in the community of those who were giving it flesh.

The message of the kingdom had become more than an idea. A new human community had sprung up and looked very much like the new order to which the evangelist has pointed. In the church, love was given daily expression; reconciliation was actually occurring; people were no longer divided into Jews and Gentiles, slave and free, male and female. In this community the weak were protected, the stranger was welcomed. People were healed, the poor and dispossessed were cared for and found justice. Everything was shared. Joy abounded and people were filled with praise.[3]

Only through the cross can we show what reconciliation looks like to the world. That kind of unity is such a source of blessing that God uses it to enable the world to believe. "I in them, and Thou in Me, that they may be perfected in unity, that the world may know that Thou didst send Me, and didst love them, even as Thou didst love me" (John 17:23).

As Gordon MacDonald said, the world can do anything the church can do except one thing: it cannot show grace. And I might add that it cannot show grace because it does not bow before the cross, where grace is given to sinners. The world can have union but not unity; it can have self-interest but not selflessness.

Christ has called us to show the way.

SEVEN

The Cross, the Basis of Moral Sanity

Morally speaking, western culture is in a free-fall. All of us are concerned about trash television, the proliferation of gay rights, pornography, and abortion on demand. Many organizations have been formed to fight these battles, using public pressure, boycotts, or legislation. After all, we agree that something needs to be done about these evils that tear at the very fabric of our families and culture.

The question, of course, is this: What should be done? We are discovering that it is difficult—if not impossible—for us to persuade pagans to live by Christian morality. For one thing, they deeply resent us "imposing our morality" upon culture as a whole. They see all restrictions as the enemy of true freedom, a kind of unrestrained freedom that they believe is their inherent "right."

And for every effort made to promote our agenda, a powerful countereffort is made to promote theirs. As I write, there is controversy about a full-page ad in a national newspaper defending the right of free speech and the need to stand against radical homosexual legislation. The media says the ad was sponsored by "a coalition of Christians." But, as we might expect, the homosexual lobby also put together a full-page ad lauding fairness and love toward homosexuals. The ad featured a touching story about the need to not stigmatize a young lesbian who was growing up in a conservative "Bible loving" family. It is difficult to know which ad had the most powerful effect. However, it's unlikely that either of them changed the mind of many readers. If anything, more sympathy was generated by the pro-homosexual ad than by the "anti-homosexual" ad, as the media dubbed it. As before, Christians were portrayed (however unfairly) as a homophobic community long on condemnation and short on love.

Second, the unbelievers among us take pleasure in pointing out any inconsistencies they can find within the evangelical community, and are convinced (whether sincerely or not) that we are nothing but self-righteous bigots who don't practice what we preach. Back in 1993 at the National Religious Broadcaster's convention Angela Lansbury was scheduled to address the delegates, but the planners debated canceling her appearance when they learned that she would be playing the role of a prostitute in an upcoming movie. When the news got out, the host of a network show could not resist remarking, "Wow! A convention of televangelists barring someone from their platform for *playing* immoral roles!"

Such a response not withstanding, we can be glad that the evangelical community stands for righteousness and opposes the glaring evils of the land. But unless we understand the deeper reasons for our nation's love affair with violence, immorality, and drugs, we will not be effective in our primary mission and will lose the moral war as well. I agree with T.S. Elliot, who wrote, "To justify Christianity because it provides a foundation for morality for the general culture instead of showing the necessity of Christian morality from the truth of Christianity is a very dangerous inversion. It is not enthusiasm but dogma that differentiates a Christian from a pagan society"[1]

We are still enjoying the benefits of our moral inertia, but the train has slowed; some would say that it has stopped altogether. The values of our forefathers have been trashed in favor of a radical individualism that fuels every fiber of human greed and self-seeking. No one knows whether the train can still make it up the hill or across the next bridge. Meanwhile, some of our social planners think that the Judeo-Christian locomotive should be taken to a museum, a relic of a bygone day.

Signs of a Downward Spiral

I need not convince you that we have lost our way. There was a day when truth, decency, and civility occupied the domain between freedom and law. Values were, for the most part, inner-directed. There was a time when many people would rather have been right than be president. Today, however, with the assault on values and character, the law must do double duty. When you read in the newspapers that the mother of a three-year-old girl received a restraining order against the three-year-old son of another mother because the toddlers could not get along in the same sandbox, that story is more than just an interesting commentary on contemporary American life. Some adults no longer find within themselves the ability to negotiate the most trivial disagreement! But in the absence of reason, character, and truth, and with the breakdown of social structures, a judge had to intervene.

On the one hand we are assaulted by a radical individualism that asserts that everyone has a right to pursue his or her own interests at the expense of others. This attitude has fueled a passionate return to a ruthless morality that affirms the autonomy of each person. But as this individualism asserts itself more and more, it must increasingly be held in check by the law. We see this in the sex scandals in our military.

On the other hand, a proliferation of movies and books promote violence, greed, and self-fulfillment at the expense of others; yet when such behavior is practiced, the law must intervene to keep society functioning. As David Wells put it, we are experiencing competition between law and freedom to occupy a middle territory: "The result is that the fires of license are stoked constantly by our growing moral relativism while at the same time they have to be constantly doused by our resort to law and government."[2]

We could have guessed that a society that nourishes 70 percent of all of the world's lawyers would eventually convert every desire into a right. All kinds of rights are now found in the constitution: reproductive rights, the right to happiness, the politically correct right to never have to listen to anything with which one disagrees, the right to group power, and so on. From these rights spin a whole host of individual complaints jamming our courts, with each person stretching the law to the limits to seek out some settlement, some windfall of profit.

Then there's the tremendous moral confusion that abounds today. You may remember reading about the young woman who secretly gave birth to a baby in a motel room with her boyfriend present. After the baby was born they crushed its skull and threw it in a dumpster. Many people were shocked that two young people who had never been in trouble before would do such a thing. Yet think about it: on the one hand the individualism of our culture advocates abortion on demand—it is permissible to kill a baby if you believe it will interfere with your personal peace and happiness. On the other hand, if you wait until the infant is born, you are charged with murder. Before birth you have a right to kill the infant, but after birth, such an act can be prosecuted to the full extent of the law.

America's moral locomotive is running on the inertia of previous generations that respected the Bible, if not believed it. There was in this nation what Francis Schaeffer called a "Christian consensus": a belief that there are absolutes, that morality is more than just a matter of personal opinion and convenience. There was a commitment to values that grew out of a Judeo-Christian view of the world. But once the Bible is rejected, pagan values are allowed to come to their natural conclusion in morality, law, and politics.

Needless to say, Christians are concerned. They are concerned about children who are taught how to be immoral in our schools; they are concerned about the violence and pornography on television, videotapes, and the internet. Millions of decent citizens are wondering how to turn the tide. Can the train be started again? What fuel can we use to fire the engine so that the ground that has been lost might be recovered?

Those who fight the battle of pornography can have an impact; there have been citizens who have worked to shut down adult shops or have pornography and X-rated films banned. We have enough existing laws on the books to put smut peddlers out of business. For this goal we can cooperate with others, whether Christian or not.

In addition, parents should unite to put restrictions on the Internet to protect their children from various kinds of obscenity. We can work to outlaw abortion and work toward fair laws in the workplace. For such enterprises we can join with those of other religions or, for that matter, no religion at all. Keep in mind that common grace is that gift of God to all men, who created all people with a conscience and a general perception of right or wrong. *But let us not replace the primary mission of the church with these kinds of political or moral pursuits.*

Gains brought about through legislation will always be minimal. Our battles will be something like trying to keep ants out of a house. If they first come in through the basement and we plug up the basement, they will come in under the door. If we plug the door, then they will come through the attic. Think of what happened during the days of prohibition—those who loved whiskey got it somewhere, someplace. In fact, circumventing the law became a challenge that was gladly accepted by those who resented any intrusion upon their freedom to drink spirits of their choice.

Unfortunately, many Christians define Christianity in moral rather than doctrinal terms. Thus when a mainline denomination chooses to ordain homosexuals, the evangelicals among them throw up their hands, shouting, "Something must be done! Our denomination has become liberal!" In point of fact, the denomination became liberal many years earlier when it no longer believed in the binding authority of the Scriptures and ceased preaching the law and gospel. The moral laxity we see around us has its roots in doctrinal error. We must never forget that it is not a disrespect for moral values but rather a disrespect for the message of the cross that lies at the heart of our cultural malaise. In short, *America has chosen the wrong morality because it has chosen to worship the wrong God.*

J. Gresham Machen (1881–1937) was a famous Bible scholar and defender of orthodox Christianity. Beginning in 1906 he taught New Testament at Princeton Theological Seminary, and in 1926 he was appointed as professor of apologetics. This appointment aroused a great deal of opposition for one reason: Machen refused to get on the bandwagon and support the prohibition movement. This movement gained much support as a moral crusade endorsed by Christians. As a result of Machen's refusal, his appointment to the chair of apologetics was prevented by the Presbyterian General Assembly. He argued that while the Bible was clear about the evils of drunkenness, it said nothing about matters related to the production and distribution of drink.

Please think this through: At the very time Machen's appointment was denied, the Presbyterian church had begun its slide into liberal theology! The church took a definite stand on the political correctness of prohibition, but not on the theological correctness of the Bible. Machen believed that the church should be theologically intolerant but politically tolerant.

The error of Christians being more concerned about moral crusades rather than doctrinal integrity has reoccurred in our time. Yes, we are in need of moral reform, but we cannot have it without doctrinal reform. Perhaps Jacques Ellul only slightly overstated the case when he said that the New Testament teaches no such thing as a Judeo-Christian ethic. "It commands conversion," he said, and then, "Be perfect, as your heavenly Father is perfect" (Matthew 5:48).

Perhaps no temptation for the church is as great as that of substituting moral reform for spiritual and doctrinal reformation. Because the moral breakdown in society is so clearly seen, because immorality is so easy to attack, and because there is a widespread consensus that something must be done, we are all too eager to settle for something far less than our biblical mandate requires.

Diagnosing the Cause of Our Moral Breakdown

Many Christians think it is easy to find the villains who are responsible for America's moral demise: Hollywood, the pornographers, liberal judges, and the radical pro-abortionists and gay rights lobbies, all supported by the American Civil Liberties Union. Many of us assume that if we vilify these obvious offenders and vote for authorities who think like we do, then we can "take this country back." Not only is such a diagnosis superficial, but so is the prescribed cure. As the church, we should think more carefully about the cause of our problems and pursue a biblical response.

The Extent of Our Need

Before we even speak about the role that laws can play in our nation, we must consider God's analysis of the human heart. The ten commandments are not merely a list of "Thou shalt nots"; they reflect for us the nature of God. The law was given not only so that Israel might try to keep it, but also so the nation might be convinced that the human heart is too sinful to obey God's precepts. *If we try to have a moral nation without being a God-fearing nation, we are building on sand.*

After a highly publicized shooting in one of our nation's schools, evangelical Christians on a talk-show program traced the problem back to the removal of prayer from public schools in 1962. Imagine! Two teenagers shot some of their classmates, and the culprit is the supreme court! The talk-show guests said the solution was to put prayer back in our schools, take America back from the humanists, and such events won't happen! But many countries in Europe still have prayer in school, and, from what I have observed, although their murder rate might be lower (in my opinion no other nation has as much of a love affair with guns as does America), their moral and spiritual darkness is greater than ours. It is simplistic to think that the answer to today's crises among young people is to simply have the teacher recite a prayer to some unnamed deity!

To see the seriousness of what is happening around us, we need to have a biblical understanding of the holiness of God. The average church-goer is like the young lawyer who told Christ very sincerely that he had kept the commandments from his youth up. He had no idea of the extent to which He had offended the holiness of God. A child who breaks a vase might think that he has not done anything serious because he thinks it is worth only a few dollars. But when he discovers that it is worth $25,000, he then begins to grasp why his disobedience was so destructive. As long as we think that God is much like we are—tolerant of sin and quite willing to overlook our transgressions—we are likely to think that redemption is helpful but not urgent. It is this lack of understanding the depth of our need that leads us to rely upon superficial solutions for our problems.

Many pastors no longer preach about God's holiness and man's depravity, arguing that we must speak to the "felt needs" of the day. Thus much contemporary preaching centers on relationships within the family, how to conquer depression, and how to have a better self-image. The focus is on how Christ can help a person be a better businessman or career woman rather than on our need to prepare for heaven and face the final judgment. We are told that if we want to be relevant, we must "scratch people where they itch."

As a result, many churches today offer a Christ who will help people become healthy, wealthy, and fulfilled. But Michael Horton writes, "Our greatest problem is that we stand under the guilty verdict in heaven, and a day is coming when that appearance in court will make this subject the most acute 'felt need' of our entire existence."[3] If the people around us have no "felt need" to be justified by God through Christ, then our responsibility is to preach the demands of God's law until they cry, "Woe is me, for I am undone."

Of course I am not saying that we preach only against other people's sin and God's impending judgment. Some people rail against homosexuals, abortionists, and the corruption in Washington. They are often angry, raining judgment upon politicians, the supreme court, and who knows what else. They consider themselves to be bold when in fact, they are stumbling blocks to the gospel, presenting a harsh, angry spirit that is foreign to the attitude of Christ. The Pharisee who congratulated himself for abstaining from the sins of the flesh and thanked God that he was not "like other men" was further from God than the publican who understood, however imperfectly, the depth of his personal sin.

We must tell the world that we stand with them under the judgment of God, apart from His undeserved grace. We cannot continually be making enemies of the very people we hope to reach with the gospel. We can only explain the depths of our sin if we are sensitive to our own need.

Theological liberals have always operated from the premise that human beings are essentially good; they assume that all that man needs is to be shown what is right and he will do it. There is no wrath of God from which we must be saved. While this same heresy might not be explicitly taught in evangelical churches, it is frequently implied by our neglect of the great themes of salvation. Think of the number of people who believe that the TV series "Touched by an Angel" is Christian when, in actuality, it never mentions sin, the cross, or Christ. The assumption promoted by the show is that angels are waiting to help anyone, no matter his theology or lifestyle. Such heresy is often found within our churches, too.

When Harry Caray—a popular sportscaster in Chicago—died, the news carried interviews with comments about him "looking down from the sky" or "finding a baseball team in heaven." If anyone had publicly suggested that his arrival in heaven would be dependent on whether he had been born again through personal faith in Christ, that person would have been contemptuously dismissed as a narrow-minded religious fanatic. Imagine making the same comment about the eternal destiny of Princess Diana or Jacqueline Kennedy! They were good people, we would be told. How dare anyone suggest that they might be en route to eternal condemnation!

Our battle is not between two competing moral systems; our battle is between two competing Gods. We cannot stoke the Christian train with morality and expect it to resume its journey along the tracks. We must once again proclaim the truth that made the church great: the fact that we are all sinners already suffering under the righteous judgment of God. If we do not flee to Christ for protection from condemnation, we shall not escape the fires of hell. We have a great deal of educating to do in a culture where only 17 percent of the people believe that sin is a violation of God's will.

I've learned that a defense of Christian morality, no matter how reasonable, will never change the minds of those who are determined to follow their own ways. The fact is, people act on the basis of what pleases them ("If it feels good, do it") and not on the basis of rational considerations. I have had to repeatedly learn that it is the transformation of heart that leads to the transformation of life. And it is that lesson which we must adhere to if we desire to see real change take place in a person's life.

The Nature of God's Cure

Savonarola, who lived in the same age as Luther, was a moral reformer who preached against the evils of the city of Florence. He was the impetus behind the "bonfire of the vanities," in which citizens did away with their lewd books, false hairdos, and gambling objects. He railed against the evils of his day, but did not clearly point men and women to Christ. Although he inspired moral reform, it did not last because it was not based on the proclamation of the gospel. He thought it was possible to have moral recovery without doctrinal recovery. He thought he could get pagans to accept family values if only he preached against the moral laxity of his time. Not so.

By contrast, Luther understood that only theological reformation would make moral reformation possible. And although he did not take the Reformation as far as many of us might have liked, there was a definite corresponding moral revival in many places where the Reformation took hold. The Reformation was begun not to change culture, but to restore the gospel that had been lost through centuries of corruption and obscure traditions. And yet, as the gospel was recovered, the door was opened to science, public education, and eventually civil liberties.

God's answer goes to the very heart of our moral crisis: First, through faith in Christ we are acquitted, declared righteous by God Himself. And second, there is an actual transformation of the human heart: "If any man is in Christ, he is a new creature; the old things passed away; behold, new things have come" (2 Corinthians 5:17). Through Christ our relationship with God is rectified and we are eternally His.

Politics cannot raise the dead or give sight to the blind. Moral reforms cannot take a heart of stone and turn it into a heart of flesh. What we cannot do through voting blocs, threats, and boycotts, God can do through the proclamation of His message. We must not be satisfied with moral reform when God commands moral transformation. God's agenda is greater, more urgent, and has eternal repercussions.

For some, the temptation to clean up society in the name of Christianity is irresistible. The great Russian writer Tolstoy undertook just such an enterprise. David Walsh quotes from Dostoyevski's book *Under the Rubble,* criticizing Tolstoy as one who fell for the temptation of moralizing the message of Christianity. Walsh adds:

> What is missing in the liberal exhortation to simple moral goodness, even as historically exemplified by the "Christianity" of Tolstoy, is an awareness of the depth of evil that tugs on the human heart. This lack of awareness fails to recognize the extent to which the thinker's reasoning itself is infected with the disease.[4]

We must not fall for this temptation. We must recover the Pauline doctrine of man's inability to do anything that pleases God in and of himself. We must look upon political or legal victories for what they are: Band-Aids that will break when we are outnumbered, outfinanced, and outsmarted in the courts of the land. We can be thankful for those who are trying to plug the hole in the dike, but what is needed more is a dam that can hold back the polluted spiritual waters that flood our land.

The Power of Prayer

In his powerful book, *Fresh Wind, Fresh Fire,* Jim Cymbala writes that he discovered an astonishing truth, "God is attracted to weakness. He can't resist those who humbly and honestly admit how desperately they need Him."[5]

Jim and his wife's commitment to lead their church in persistent, continual prayer has given the Brooklyn Tabernacle spiritual inroads into the city of New York. On Tuesday evenings, the church is crowded as hundreds come to pray and share specific answers to prayer. Through this humble witness, thousands of people have come to know Christ as Savior and have been delivered from homosexuality, prostitution, and drugs. God has continually provided funds for a greater building as the crowds come to see the power of God at work. Today the ministry of the Brooklyn Tabernacle Choir is known throughout the United States, a tribute to the fact that God answers prayer.

We cannot possibly predict what might happen if all of the evangelical churches in America had a similar commitment to prayer and fasting. Imagine the credibility that the church would gain if we had tens of thousands of changed lives to validate the power of the gospel. All of this could be done without antagonizing the political structures, without trying to outvote or outshout our opponents. Cymbala writes, "The devil is not terribly frightened of our human efforts and credentials. But he knows his kingdom will be damaged when we begin to lift our hearts to God."[6]

Nor is the devil afraid of our political involvement. He knows that political victories cannot directly promote the kingdom of God. More people are not converted, nor is our witness more powerful because we have elected the right people to represent us. What is more, any "Christian" victories might be overturned in the next election. Only what is done for Christ has eternal repercussions that can never be lost. The message of the cross, no matter how seemingly insignificant, brings more permanent change than the most lauded political victory.

The Task at Hand

Ancient Corinth was, in some respects, a city just like many found in America. There was rampant immorality—every form of homosexuality, abuse, and adultery. This city reflected the morality of the Roman Empire, of which is said that 14 out of the first 15 emperors were either homosexuals or bisexuals. Even as

Paul was writing his first letter to the church at Corinth, Nero was planning to marry the boy Sporus. The Roman Empire was given over to sensuality; it is little wonder the church found it difficult to survive.

Unfortunately, the pagan culture in Corinth was reflected in the church, and the church leaders would not deal with it. Paul wrote, "It is actually reported that there is immorality among you, and immorality of such a kind as does not exist even among the Gentiles, that someone has his father's wife" (1 Corinthians 5:1). This man was sexually involved with his stepmother, and the church would not confront the issue.

If we want to clean up America, this is where we should begin: with the people of God. We must humbly affirm that every sin found in the world is also found in the church. Divorce, abortion, alcoholism, homosexuality, pornography, dishonesty—all of these are tolerated in too many churches today. Thus the salt has lost its savor, and the light is flickering.

Of course within the church we have people who have been converted out of all kinds of sinful lifestyles. But true conversion is accompanied by a change in lifestyle. Even though these people may continue to struggle with many of the sins of their past, they now dislike those sins. They view their lives from an entirely different perspective. They now have a love for God, and they yearn to do what is right despite their problems.

Notice that Paul rebuked sin within the church, but he had nothing to say about those who are outside of the church. He pointedly tells us that outsiders should be treated differently. While believers should not fellowship with disobedient people within the church, that does not mean we should cease to interact with unbelievers.

Paul's words deserve a careful reading:

I wrote you in my letter not to associate with immoral people; I did not at all mean with the immoral people of this world, or with the covetous and swindlers, or with idolaters; for then you would have to go out of the world. But I actually wrote to you to not associate with any so-called brother if he should be an immoral person, or covetous, or an idolater, or a reviler, or a drunkard, or a swindler—not even to eat with such a one. For what have I to do with judging outsiders? Do you not judge those who are within the church? But those who are outside, God judges. Remove the wicked man from among yourselves (1 Corinthians 5:9-13).

But those who are outside, God judges!

These words should be chiseled on the hearts and minds of all of the Christian activists who think that we can change society by railing against it with legislation, marches, and crusades designed to return us to the morality of another era. Even if we are politically organized, we as a minority cannot change the moral views of the majority. Again I cannot emphasize too strongly that we have a higher calling. We are called to clean up the church and to preach the gospel to the unconverted.

Paul's point is that there are some forms of behavior that should not be tolerated among those who claim to be Christians. For one church member to commit immorality has a much larger negative effect than his actions might indicate: "A little leaven leavens the whole lump" (1 Corinthians 5:6). A tablespoon of yeast is sufficient to cause a whole lump of dough to rise. Similarly, one man's sin is sufficient to poison a whole congregation. Sin cannot be sealed off; it cannot be quarantined. It is like burning incense in a dormitory room: no matter how many towels you put under the door, the smell soon wafts its way into the hallway, up the elevator, and to the rooms upstairs.

If you think this is unfair, remember that the opposite is also true: a righteous body of people can have a greater impact on their culture than their size would warrant. If a little leaven leavens the whole lump, then it is also true that a righteous congregation can have an impact far beyond its numbers. Both evil and righteousness have the power to reproduce themselves.

Paul also chided the Corinthian church for allowing its members to take one another to court before Gentile judges: "I say this to your shame. Is it so, that there is not among you one wise man who will be able to decide between his brethren, but brother goes to law with brother, and that before unbelievers?" (6:5,6). Ours is not the first litigious society. When the Corinthian believers were going to court against one another, they were looking to unbelievers for the kind of wisdom that should exist within the church itself. Paul said that they should settle their own disputes, and if they couldn't, then they should be willing to surrender their own rights for the greater good of the witness of the church. Even if they should win, he said, they would lose: "Actually, then, it is already a defeat for you, that you have lawsuits with one another. Why not rather be wronged? Why not rather be defrauded?" (verse 7).

As Christians, it is not our responsibility to right every wrong that has been done against us. Christ had His rights violated, and we should expect that to happen to us as well. When we insist on our rights—when we whine like the world until we get what we believe is our due—we lose our credibility. From the outside it looks as if we no more trust in God than the unbelievers who feel they have to get justice now because they think you only live once.

Living in the Power of the Cross

As for the power of the cross lived out in the lives of the church members at Corinth, Paul continues both to rebuke and encourage: "Do you not know that the unrighteous shall not inherit the kingdom of God? Do not be deceived; neither fornicators, nor idolaters, nor adulterers, nor effeminate, nor homosexuals, nor thieves, nor the covetous, nor drunkards, nor revilers, nor swindlers, shall inherit the kingdom of God" (1 Corinthians 6:9,10). In that list Paul mentions five sins of the flesh and five sins of the spirit.

He continues, "Such were some of you; but you were washed, but you were sanctified, but you were justified in the name of the Lord Jesus Christ, and in the Spirit of our God" (verse 11). Not all the believers had been promiscuous, but many of them had various kinds of immorality in their past. They had been addicts, indulging themselves with every sensual desire. And yet Paul speaks of this as their *past* behavior. They were converted out of that lifestyle.

Let's look now at each aspect of what took place in their conversion.

"You were washed"

Imagine a clean conscience. The answers the world has for guilt will never satisfy. First we are told to sublimate it—to think of ways to make guilt feelings go away. It is best to ignore them—just disregard the warning signals. Keep doing what you want to do and learn to live with the consequences. Accept what you have done as part of human failure and move on, rationalizing that the people we have hurt have to work through their own "karma."

My wife has a digital alarm clock that beeps every hour. Try as we might, we could not get the beeper to shut off. So we put the clock in my study, and for six months I heard it beep every hour. Eventually the sound grew faint, and now it beeps no more. The same happens to the conscience if we violate it often enough. In time, we can hurt others without a twinge of regret or guilt.

The second answer to sublimating guilt is to smother it with alcohol and drugs. This deadens the pain; it makes people who should feel bad feel quite good. Those who resort to such substances come to depend on them, for they do not want the guilt that interferes with their pleasure to stand in the way of that pleasure. A person needs to do what he needs to do, they reason.

By contrast, God offers a genuine washing of the conscience. We're not talking about a mere psychological theory; our sins are actually removed from us, thrown "into the depths of the sea" (Micah 7:19). Guilt is not a feeling that has to be unlearned; it is a feeling that is actually removed by God so that fellowship with Him is possible and the self-hatred and anger toward others can end.

Since Christ forgave me even when I treated Him unjustly, I can do the same in relation to others. When I have been redeemed and I know that I am already forgiven, then I am free to forgive others.

"You were sanctified"

Those who once sinned so greatly yet have received Christ as Savior have been set aside and labeled, "Special to God." To be sanctified is to be "set apart for the Almighty." This is God's work; no man can set himself apart for God. Of course the Christians who once indulged in the sins that Paul lists in 1 Corinthians 6:9,10 will still have struggles; those who have been converted out of the spiritual mire will have a propensity to return to their former lifestyles. The difference now is that they don't have to. Indeed, the obligation they had to obey the impulses of the body has now been set aside through Christ.

"You were justified"

Those who come to Christ are declared as righteous as God Himself is. Their sin was transferred to Christ and His righteousness was given to them. Sinners though they were, they are rightly related to God.

Think of what this message means to a child molester! Here is a human being who can scarcely live with himself, knowing that he has ruined the lives of others. Yet he too can be washed, sanctified, and justified. He too can enter heaven through the front door. We have the privilege of reminding people that there is more grace in God's present than there is sin in their past.

How Can We Bring About Change?

The message of the cross is the fuel that can restart the engine; the cross is the fuel and the Holy Spirit is the lighter that sparks the fire. Only with the fervency of Christ's love burning within our hearts and the gospel message can we ever hope to change the culture. To opt for a political or cultural transformation is like trying to push the train in our own strength. We need to kindle the fire in the engine.

What is God saying to us? We can best clean up the world by cleaning up the church. Paul had nothing to say to the pagan culture of his day except that unbelievers should repent. There was little use telling unbelievers that they should reform society, shut down the temple of prostitution, and get on with family values. He knew that the problem was much deeper—it was not a matter of reformation, but transformation.

Of course we should lead the world to a higher standard of morality by our own personal conduct, but there is little use trying to get unsaved people to accept our values. From a secular perspective, we should not be surprised that the world wants to follow its appetites wherever they happen to lead.

How can we expect the citizens of the city of man to live according to the dictates of the city of God unless they have become members of that kingdom? As long as they are members of the kingdom of darkness, that darkness will appear as light to them. Perhaps nowhere is this more clearly seen than in the killing of preborn infants. Once upon a time many of us believed that we could rationally persuade the world of the error of abortion. If only we could show them that medically, philosophically, and logically the killing of a preborn infant was to commit infanticide. We thought that if we showed them pictures of a dismembered child and proved that the preborn infant can actually feel pain, they would say, "Why of course you are right ... abortion is murder after all."

Although a few have listened with an open mind and have changed their opinion, the vast majority of those who call themselves pro-choice have chosen to ignore the evidence and plunge ahead, advocating abortion at any time for any reason. Clearly this is a position based not on reason but on the deeply cherished convictions that people should be free to engage in immorality without having to accept the consequences of having a child, or that a woman should not have to bear the child if it's going to ruin her lifestyle. To those who blindly equate freedom for women as the right to kill the unborn infant, no argument will persuade them otherwise.

I'm sure you have met people, as I have, who were on the forefront of the pro-abortion debate but became converted and changed their view to become pro-life. Homosexual radicals have been converted from pushing their agenda to ministering the grace of Christ to their communities. And it wasn't because of persuasive arguments, but rather a change of heart.

I'm not suggesting that we stop educating the world about the irrationality of abortion or the destructive nature of homosexuality. I believe that we should increase—not decrease—our discussion and persuasion. As I've said before, we can appeal to common grace—the belief that a semblance of morality exists in all humans because they are created in the image of God. But our results will be limited and subject to reversal, court orders, and the like. Remember, the human mind is able to rationalize anything that the human heart desires to do. Only a change of heart will bring about a change of mind.

Only God's light can conquer the darkness.

EIGHT

The Cross:
Standing Out in the World

Nietzsche, the philosopher who paved the way for Hitler by proclaiming "the death of God" and predicting the coming of a superman who would return Germany to greatness by force, wrote scathing denunciations of Christianity. In one outburst of rage against the church of his day he said sarcastically, "I might believe in their Redeemer if they looked more redeemed!"

Perhaps Nietzsche had no right to ask Christians to look like their Redeemer since he so vehemently hated the very values their

Redeemer espoused in His Sermon on the Mount. Nietzsche believed that love and tolerance were *not* exactly what Germany needed. It would not be the meek who would inherit the earth, but the vengeful and powerful.

But, such inconsistencies aside, Neitzsche's quote is a forceful reminder that if we want people to believe in our Redeemer, we most assuredly should look redeemed. Which should lead us to ask: What makes Christians stand out in the world? At what points should we be most unlike the world? What does it mean to carry our cross in an age in which the cross has been emptied of its meaning?

The cross represents a great "value reversal": it stands as a permanent witness to the fact that what men hate God loves, and what He loves men hate. The cross should make us recognizable in the world. Bearing our cross should be the one indisputable mark of a redeemed life. We may think the world is indifferent, but it's not. The world is watching.

If you have ever trekked through a desert, you know how surprising it is to come across a lush, fruit-bearing tree in the middle of miles of barren sand. The contrast makes you stop and take note; you know that there must be an underground stream, unseen by the human eye, but nevertheless present to grant the gift of life. The more barren the desert, the more attractive the green tree.

When the world sees us they should be surprised, taken aback, and forced to take note. We should live as though from another country, with a different set of values, different aspirations, and a different interpretation of life itself. Just as Christ was both loved and hated, both obeyed and reviled, so we should expect the same. "Remember the word that I said to you, 'A slave is not greater than his master.' If they persecuted Me, they will also persecute you; if they kept My word, they will keep yours also"

(John 15:20). We cannot demand that our political system should be Bible-friendly.

We cannot understand what the cross should mean for us unless we first understand what it meant for Christ. Indeed, at no point is He so clearly our example as when the nails pierced His hands and feet. "For you have been called for this purpose, since Christ also suffered for you, leaving you an example for you to follow in His steps, Who committed no sin, nor was any deceit found in His mouth; and while being reviled, He did not revile in return; while suffering, He uttered no threats, but kept entrusting Himself to Him who judges righteously" (1 Peter 2:21-23).

The Great Descent

Christ's descent from heaven to earth represents the greatest act of condescension. He embarked on a slope that would take Him from the heights to the depths. And if we represent Him well, we will follow in His footsteps.

Let us consider how far down Christ came, and then we will better understand our role in the world. Perhaps the greatest passage on this condescension is Philippians 2:5-8.

He Became a Servant

In Philippians 2:5-7, Paul wrote, "Have this attitude in yourselves which was also in Christ Jesus, who, although He existed in the form of God, did not regard equality with God a thing to be grasped, but emptied Himself, taking the form of a bond-servant, and being made in the likeness of men." Christ existed in the form (Greek=*morphe*) of God, and He became the form (*morphe*) of a servant.

In heaven Christ gave orders; on earth He would receive them. He who had received the adulation of the heavenly hosts would be mocked, falsely accused, and sometimes ignored. He who owned all things would not have a suit of clothes He could call His own.

To understand the extent of the descent, we must remember that at the Council of Nicea in 325 A.D. the delegates debated whether Christ had a similar essence or the very same essence as God the Father. The conclusion was that He was "God of very God," that He was of the *same* substance as the Father. When Paul writes that Christ existed "in the form of God" he means that Christ has the very essence of God. As someone once said, "He really is God; He is not just applying for the job!"

What might Jesus have looked like if we could have seen Him before Bethlehem? Isaiah saw Him and wrote, "In the year of King Uzziah's death, I saw the Lord sitting on a throne, lofty and exalted, with the train of His robe filling the temple" (6:1). Angels surrounded the throne, calling to each other, "Holy Holy Holy, is the LORD of hosts, the whole earth is full of His glory" (verse 3).

We might be tempted to say that this is a description of God the Father, not God the Son. But the apostle John does not allow us to make such an assumption. He quotes Isaiah's response to this vision and then adds, "These things Isaiah said, because he saw His glory, and he spoke of *Him*" (John 12:41, emphasis added). Christ was the one on the throne; Christ was the one for whom the angels sang.

This equality with God was not something at which Christ "grasped"—that is, He did not hold onto His position, insisting on His right to enjoy heaven without interruption. He "emptied Himself" and became a servant. He didn't volunteer to be God, but He did volunteer to be a servant.

That He emptied Himself cannot mean that He gave up His attributes, for then He would have ceased to be God. Rather, it means that He chose to not depend upon His divine attributes. By way of illustration, suppose you were a millionaire yet you chose to live in the ghetto. You go to work with the poor, eat with them, and work as hard as they. At any moment you could leave the ghetto and live in splendor, but you choose to not depend upon your personal resources. In the same way, Christ gave up the independent use of His attributes so that He might be an authentic servant.

Christ was *omnipotent* yet we read, "Jesus therefore, being wearied from His journey, was sitting thus by the well" (John 4:6). Christ was *omniscient* and yet we read "Of that day or hour no one knows, not even the angels in heaven, nor the Son, but the Father alone" (Mark 13:32). Christ was *omnipresent*, for He told Nicodemus that the Son of Man "is in heaven." Yet we read, "When therefore He [Christ] heard that he [Lazarus] was sick, He stayed then two days longer in the place where He was" (John 11:6).

In order to be a servant, Christ had to live as a man in dependence upon the Father. He said that He did nothing by His own initiative and strength, but did only what the Father wanted Him to do. It was all voluntary, of course, for He still possessed the attributes of deity.

Christ did not have to accept such humiliation and the abuse that went along with it. He didn't leave the courts of heaven because He was fired; He was not squeezed out because of a restructuring move within the Godhead. He *chose* the downward slope.

Now He was shouted at: "Get out of the way!" or, "We know who you are—a carpenter's son!" He sometimes walked 50 miles in one week, often with scant supplies and virtually no protection from the weather. This was not the role to which He was accustomed.

He did not have to let a mob try to push Him from the brow of a hill.

He did not have to put up with the treachery of Judas and the broken promises of His disciples.

He did not have to accept abuse from Herod and the Roman soldiers.

We can't understand this. We tend to hold a firm grip on position and power until our knuckles turn white. We fight when we are demoted; we claim our rights and threaten legal action. We gossip and criticize and try to manipulate people and circumstances in order to "even the score." We become angry and resentful; we argue and plead.

I know of a man in a Christian organization who simply was not up to the task that was expected of him. Month after month he could point to no accomplishments. Each week he came to his boss armed with a pack of excuses and promises. When he was asked to resign or be fired, he hired an attorney and sued his fellow brothers for job discrimination. Never mind that the Bible expressly forbids such action; never mind that his job performance rating was so meager. Never mind that he should have known he deserved it! Here was a man who claimed to be redeemed but he was as unlike his Redeemer as it is possible to be.

Christ, by contrast, left His position in heaven to assume a position which was unnatural to Him. He voluntarily laid aside His own prerogatives so that he might help us. He humbled Himself when He had nothing to be humble about. In short, He stepped down the ladder when He ruled at the top.

The world does not have many opportunities to see us as servants. We must do all we can to meet the needs of suffering people. We must, like Christ, be seen walking among the people of the world, doing good. We should go to great lengths to not polarize the very people who need to hear the message we have to share.

He Changed His Appearance

Christ had the "form" of God, and He took the "form" of a servant and was "made in the likeness of men." That word "likeness" should not be interpreted to mean that He only *appeared* as if He were a man; no, He actually was a man. He had the essence of God and the essence of man. He united both in one person.

Someone once said that those little hands that created the world would themselves have to be held. The feet that had traveled throughout the length and breadth of the universe—the feet whose "going forth were from old, even from everlasting"—would have to learn to walk. The eyes that were like a flame of fire and could pierce every particle in the universe would have to adjust to the dim light of a stable. And the ears that heard the whispers of the universe would have to learn to listen. The tongue that spoke and brought forth light would have to learn to speak Aramaic and Hebrew.

In heaven, no one asked who was sitting upon the throne. On earth, He traveled unrecognized, having to show His I.D. His mysterious birth elicited the derision of His peers, and His father's humble occupation as a carpenter was used to discredit His teachings.

Many men have aspired to become gods; indeed, the Romans took their emperors and declared them to be gods. But only once in history did a God aspire to become a man.

He Changed His Roles

Christ went from Victor to Victim.

He was "obedient to the point of death, even death on a cross" (Philippians 2:8). There were many ways to die and crucifixion was reserved for the bad guys. It was the chosen method for the criminals, the rabble-rousers. It was a curse to hang on a cross. Christ was so cursed.

From the crown to the cross. From being in charge to letting others take charge. From controlling the devil to choosing to let the devil be in control. He looked His enemies in the eye and said, "Today, you win." And yet with such humility, He changed the world.

Christ did not use political power to bring change. He did not usher in a kingdom in which the subjects would have to obey; that kingdom is yet future. Rather, He chose to concentrate on the hidden kingdom—the transformation of lives. And so should we.

Looking Redeemed

What do we learn from this "reversal of values"?

First, *God's way up is down.* "You younger men, likewise, be subject to your elders; and all of you, clothe yourselves with humility toward one another, for God is opposed to the proud, but gives grace to the humble. Humble yourselves, therefore, under the mighty hand of God, that He may exalt you at the proper time" (1 Peter 5:5,6). God elevates those who surrender their rights; He honors those who take up their cross as Christ did. And for us, as for Him, the cross is the way of death.

We have something to be humble about! We are sinners. We must come to the place where we realize that whatever good there is in us is implanted by God.

If we are as selfish as the world—if we angrily insist on our rights and make a spectacle of the insults we receive, either real or imagined—we will be indistinguishable from our culture. The world is not impressed when we malign them with overtones of political self-interest. Remember, at the end of the day, what the world needs most is to see Jesus.

That does not mean that we roll over and play dead when we are discredited, lied about, and have our rights violated. We can protest and argue our case, but we should do so with a loving spirit and a caring heart. We should willingly endure injustice with dignity because we see it as a badge of honor. "For this finds favor, if for the sake of conscience toward God a man bears up under sorrows when suffering unjustly. For what credit is there if, when you sin and are harshly treated, you endure it with patience—But if when you do what is right and suffer for it you patiently endure it, this finds favor with God" (1 Peter 2:19,20). To have God's approval is the highest quest of those who are in touch with the highest reality.

After a Promise Keeper's rally in Atlanta a number of years ago, hundreds of us pastors took trains to return to our hotels. Upon arriving at the train station, we were to take vans that would shuttle us back to our hotels. Unfortunately, a van came only every few minutes, and given the large number of us, the wait was long. It was late in the evening and a cold wind was blowing. The whole time, all eyes were glued to the street to see when the next van would come. And when it arrived, everyone wanted to be the first to jump in! What a sight to see pastors who teach the need to "prefer others better than themselves" all jockeying for the best position to get into a van!

I was bothered by what happened. Yes, it was a small matter, but it proved that even those of us who supposedly "walk with God" still tend to put ourselves first when we're in difficult circumstances. Once I was finally able to get into a van, I remarked, "Whatever the filling of the Spirit means, it evidently does not mean that we prefer someone else above ourselves." The flesh dies hard.

The second thing we learn from Christ's "reversal of values" is that *the world is changed by suffering.* Christ did not change the world through His miracles, but by His suffering. Likewise, only our suffering will change the world. We think that if we had the power to do miracles we would be able to change the world. Christ had that power and He did change the world for a few people, but they too had to die. But when He wanted to do the greater miracle—when He wanted to accomplish the grand plan of redemption—only suffering brought about the desired result.

Now, there are different kinds of suffering.

There is the suffering of circumstances. Job pleased God because of how he initially endured his trial. Later he had doubts and complaints, but when he lost his children he worshiped rather than cursed. Job's attitude pleased God. For some people suffering comes from marriage conflict, for others suffering comes from failing health or an accident. While we are perfected in suffering, suffering is not "bearing our cross" because the same difficulties are found in the lives of those who spurn the cross.

There is also the suffering of persecution—the suffering that comes because of our willingness to be identified with Christ. "Bearing our cross" refers to the suffering we endure because we are Christians. This suffering calls for us to endure injustice and accept what comes from God's hands. William Barclay wrote, "We must never think of the cross as our penalty, but as our glory." When we expend ourselves for others, that is a picture of Christ in the world.

There is a third kind of suffering: that of voluntarily identifying with those who suffer. In this kind of suffering we take upon ourselves other people's burdens—burdens that we could easily avoid. This is the suffering of those who identified with the Jews during World War II when they could have remained silent, the suffering chosen by the person who adopts an especially needy child, the suffering of the one who sacrifices his career for the challenge of missionary work in a remote jungle tribe. Chosen suffering, I believe, is most precious to God. Dietrich Bonhoeffer wrote, "When Christ calls a man, He bids him 'come and die.' " At the age of 39 Bonhoeffer died. He knew that the path he chose for his life would lead to suffering, yet he did not avoid it. What about us? Someday Christ will say:

> "Depart from Me, accursed ones, into the eternal fire which has been prepared for the devil and his angels; for I was hungry, and you gave Me nothing to eat; I was thirsty, and you gave Me nothing to drink; I was a stranger, and you did not invite Me in; naked, and you did not clothe Me; sick, and in prison, and you did not visit Me." Then they themselves also will answer, saying "Lord, when did we see You hungry, or thirsty, or a stranger, or naked, or sick, or in prison, and did not take care of you?" Then He will answer them, saying, "Truly, I say to you, to the extent that you did not do it to one of the least of these, you did not do it to Me" (Matthew 25:41-45).

I grieve when I see the innkeeper at Bethlehem badly portrayed in sermons and Christmas pageants. He is credited with turning away Mary, who bore the Son of God. But think about it: he did not know who Mary was, nor about the divine child she carried in her womb. As far as he was concerned, Mary and Joseph were just one more peasant couple who had the misfortune of having nowhere to spend the night. And, besides, have you ever thought of how irritated guests would be if they were asked to give up their room for someone else, even for a pregnant woman?

What the innkeeper did ignorantly, we do deliberately. We turn Christ away by refusing our hearts and our homes to "the least of these." If Christ were to appear in one of our churches and the members had the opportunity of inviting Him into their homes, you can imagine the fight people would have to be first and to keep Him the longest. Yet we have the opportunity to invite Christ in our home every day of the week. Seldom do we accept His overtures.

Bonhoeffer asked his generation, "Who is Jesus Christ for us?" For him, it was the Jews in danger of Hitler's "final solution." They were Christ to him.

Who is Christ for us?

- the unborn child and the terrified teenager who knows not where to turn

- the single mother who needs someone to give her son a male bonding experience

- the biracial child who is ridiculed because of his or her features

- the homosexual who is so overwhelmed with guilt that he is contemplating suicide

- the inmates in a local prison who have no one to visit them

- the poor in our inner cities

These are Christ to us today. But so is our alderman, the president, the mayor, and the cab driver. Everyone whom we are quick to criticize is Christ for us today.

Ed Dobson says that the church cannot allow itself to be dominated by political action; the accent "must always be on what can be done to meet the needs of suffering people; it must be an invitation to those with political power to work with us to solve problems and help people lift themselves above circumstances."[1]

At a religious festival in Brazil there was a sign that read, "Cheap Crosses for Sale." Just so, we often want a cross that is easy to carry—a cross that does not require us to scale down our lifestyle. We are looking for a bargain. But only the cross of Christ will do if we are to accept Nietzsche's challenge.

Accepting the Full Weight of the Cross

There is a story about a pilgrim making his way to the Promised Land. He was carrying his master's cross, a burden he cheerfully accepted. However, he noticed that the further he walked, the heavier it became. As the pilgrim became weary, he sat down to rest and noticed a woodsman nearby. "Good friend," the pilgrim called, "could I use your axe to shorten my cross?" The woodsman complied.

The pilgrim traveled on, making much progress. The cross was shorter, his burden lighter. Soon the Promised Land was in sight. Drawing near, however, he noticed that a deep gulf separated him from the glories beyond. He would use the cross to span the chasm.

Though he struggled mightily to span the divide with the cross, it fell short by the very amount he had removed. Just then the pilgrim awoke; it was just a dream. And now with tears streaming down his face, he clutched his cross to his breast and pressed on. The cross was just as heavy, but its burden was lighter. Of course I need not point out that we do not enter heaven by "carrying our heavy cross" but by trusting in Christ for our salvation. But that said, we are to carry our cross if we are to have an abundant entrance into the Promised Land. Blessed are those who carry its full weight!

There are many things we can do as we see the persecution of Christians on the rise. We can organize politically, we can angrily denounce our enemies, or we can prudently choose to carry our cross—all of it. *The lighter our cross, the weaker our witness.*

Bishop Samuel, who died in a hail of gunfire with Anwar Sadat of Egypt back in the early 1980s told Dr. Ray Bakke how Christianity captured northern Africa in the early centuries. He spoke about the love of the Christians that defied explanation. For example, in those days there were no abortion procedures, so unwanted children were just left to die on the streets. And since there were no baby bottles, nursing mothers gathered in the town square. Then there would be "baby runs"—young men seeking abandoned infants. These were brought to the nursing mothers, who adopted them as their own.

Also, because Christians were often discriminated against, they were given lowly positions in the work force—many of them were garbage collectors. When the Christians came across dead bodies (often as the result of a plague), they would wash the bodies and give them a decent burial, arguing that even the wicked deserve a burial in light of the coming resurrection. It was such acts of love that stimulated the minds of the pagans: they were impressed by a supernatural love, a love of service even to the people of the world. It was with their hearts that believers won north Africa to the Christian faith.

Yes … Nietzsche, for all of his insanities, had one thing right: If Christians expect people to believe in their Redeemer, they are going to have to look more redeemed. And standing at the center of this redemption is accepting the cross as a way of life. We must remember the words of Bonhoeffer: "It is not before us, but before the cross that the world trembles."

NINE

The Triumph
of the Crucified

"What will happen to the kingdom of God if Clinton is elected?" a Christian activist asked back in 1992. Given what we have learned in this book, the answer we would have given him would be, "The kingdom of God might do very well, thank you."

Not until we understand the difference between the kingdom of God and the kingdom of man will we escape the pessimism that so often characterizes those who see the demise of God's kingdom in every downward turn of human events. Yes, the kingdom of God did quite well even under the likes of Nero, and more recently under Mao Tse-tung after the communist victory in China in 1949. When Christ said that He would build His church and the gates of Hades would not prevail against it, we can be sure that nothing—not even electing the "wrong" president—can thwart God's purposes.

We must remember that the church does not need political structures to keep it propped up. Certainly God uses the economic, social, and political powers of the day to further His purposes, but at times the church has had to survive on its own while surrounded by a hostile culture and government. We are heartened by the words of C.S. Lewis: "Nations, cultures, arts, civilization—these are mortal, and their life is to ours as the life of a gnat."[1]

We have learned that our responsibility is to share the good news of the cross before the watching world. But why should we be optimistic about the eventual outcome? The answer is that Christ is indeed Lord of the kingdoms, even today. And there is no event that so portrays the triumph of Christ than His ascension into heaven.[2]

Given the curtain that divides us from the hereafter, it is not surprising that the sacred writings of virtually all the leading religions are silent about the present responsibilities of their dead leaders. The most devout Moslem will admit that he really does not know what Mohammed has been doing during these many centuries, though he is believed to be in paradise. Hindus can only guess what role Krishna plays on the other side of the grave. The same goes for the followers of Bahaullah, Zoroaster, and others. Not only is the present existence of these leaders unclear, but so are their plans for the future.

The Significance of Christ's Ascension

Christ, as God in the flesh, was raised from the dead to confirm His predictions. He is the only person qualified to tell us what lies on the other side of death. Given these credentials, we should not be surprised that we not only have details about His bodily ascension into heaven, but a description of what He is doing today and what His plans are for tomorrow. He is a leader who is now consciously in charge and will rule over the affairs of this world even more directly in the future. Ultimately, He is King not just over the city of God, but also the city of man. He has no serious rivals in the universe. But I'm ahead of the story.

Let's read Luke's account:

> After He had said these things, He was lifted up while they were looking on, and a cloud received Him out of their sight. And as they were gazing intently into the sky while He was departing, behold, two men in white clothing stood beside them; and they also said, "Men of Galilee, why do you stand looking into the sky? This Jesus, who has been taken up from you into heaven, will come in just the same way as you have watched Him go into heaven?" (Act 1:9-11).

Christ went up—that is, His body actually left the earth and He entered the atmospheric heavens. He disappeared in a cloud. He took a journey that involved space and time; His body did not vanish, it moved upward from the Mount of Olives until it disappeared beyond human sight. He actually "passed through the heavens" (Hebrews 4:14).

This event has been ridiculed because, we are told, it is contrary to a modern scientific understanding of the universe. The ancients believed in a three-leveled universe, with heaven above, the flat earth in the middle, and hell below. Since the time of Copernicus we have known that the earth is round and therefore what is an upward movement in the Middle East would be a downward movement in New Zealand. Or to state the objection differently, to the people on the other side of the world Christ's ascension would have been a "decension" of sorts into regions unknown.

In reply we must remember that the Bible describes heaven as both a place and a state. As a place, it is the very dwelling place of God; it could be far beyond the stellar universe. Biblically, we know that there are three heavens: 1) the atmosphere, 2) the stellar universe, and 3) the abode of angels, the dwelling place of God. When Paul said Christ passed "far above all the heavens" (Ephesians 4:10), he wanted us to grasp as best we can the awesome position Christ now holds. Where that is we do not know, for after He went into the cloud, He may not have continued to travel in a straight line. We must be satisfied to know that Christ went to the central dwelling place of the Almighty.

As a state, heaven represents an entirely different order of reality. Its occupants can apparently traverse great distances in an instant, unhindered by the spatial limitations that inhibit our travel plans. At the ascension, Jesus went from one mode of existence to another: from the material world to the spiritual world, from the finite world to the infinite world. We don't know the coordinates of heaven, but we can say—thanks to eyewitnesses—that Jesus left this earth gradually, visibly, and bodily.

The return of Christ to heaven changed the character of heaven forever. His arrival marked the first time perfect humanity had ever entered the presence of God. He was the first man in heaven with a resurrected body. When the believers of the Old Testament died, their body went to the grave and their souls either went to Sheol (as some believe) or to heaven. Either way, they do not yet have their permanent resurrected body, for the resurrection of the dead is yet future. (Enoch and Elijah had unusual disappearances; it would, however, be strange indeed if, contrary to all others, they already have their resurrection body.)

Of this we can be certain: Never before had Christ been in heaven joined to a human body. Never before had there been a man with nail prints at the center of the universe. Christ had resided in heaven before, but not as the God-man. On earth He had prayed to His Father, "Glorify Thou Me together with Thyself, Father, with the glory which I had with Thee before the world was" (John 17:5). Now he had returned to a direct manifestation of that former glory. Today Christ, in perfect manhood, is in the midst of the throne seated in the heavens. His glory is like that which was seen on the Mount of Transfiguration; He is ablaze with blinding light.

At Christ's arrival the angels were most likely confounded. They had studied God's plan of redemption and were astounded at His wonder, love, and power. They had pondered God's descent to sinful humanity; yet, considered in another way, they saw His humiliation as a visual demonstration of God's indescribable love and grace. In fact, there would not have been an ascent if there had not first been a descent that accomplished the divine purpose. Yes, Christ had occupied this exalted position before, but the ascension was proof that He had accomplished His mission. The ascension, in the words of F.B. Meyer, "set an eternal seal upon the victory won in the mystery and darkness of the descent." Upon Christ's return, they assuredly sang, "Holy, holy is the Lord God of hosts, earth and heaven are filled with His glory!"

Even before His death, Christ had, in effect, told the disciples that the Son of Man would ascend (John 6:62). The ascension was a necessary confirmation of His successful mission on earth. Augustine said, "Unless the Savior had ascended to heaven, his nativity would have come to nothing.... His passion would have borne no fruit for us and His most holy resurrection would have been useless."

The Rights of the Son of God

This arrival of Christ in heaven signified that He had the following rights:

The Right to Ownership

When the God-man stepped back into the glories of heaven, no one questioned His right to enter. He did not come pleading for mercy. No mediator opened the door for Him. He was not seeking a privilege that was beyond His rights. He was simply returning home after a painful but successful journey.

Why did He own this honor?

First, because of who He is. The presence of His human body does not obscure His divine nature. Let us remember that He is the one who created the heavens: "By Him all things were created, both in the heavens and on earth, visible and invisible, whether thrones or dominions or rulers or authorities—all things have been created by Him and for Him" (Colossians 1:16). The earth was created by Him and for Him! The heavens were created by Him and for Him! The angels who attend His every move were created by Him and for Him! No wonder He didn't simply enter heaven but strode into it as its rightful owner and heir.

What does Paul mean when he says Christ ascended to "fill all things" (Ephesians 4:10)? It may simply mean that He fills all things by His presence, His sovereignty, His activity. We are told by some that the universe is infinite, but logically we have to say that Christ (Jehovah) is greater than the universe. The creation could never be as great as the creator. He "upholds all things by the word of His power" (Hebrews 1:3). His exaltation to this position of prominence was simply a return to the glory He had before creation, the glory He enjoyed before Bethlehem. He returned to the position that was His eternal right.

Second, He had a right to heaven because of what He had done. He had carried out the responsibility which He and the Father, in eternity past, had agreed He would do. The night before He was betrayed, He told His Father, "I glorified Thee on the earth, having accomplished the work which Thou hast given Me to do" (John 17:4). And what was that work? "When He had made purification of sins, He sat down at the right hand of the Majesty on high; having become as much better than the angels, as He has inherited a more excellent name than they" (Hebrews 1:3,4).

As God, Christ was perfect, yet we are told "He learned obedience from the things which He suffered. And having been made perfect, He became to all those who obey Him the source of eternal salvation" (Hebrews 5:8,9). When Christ returned to heaven, He was not simply perfect as the Son of God, but also perfect as the Son of Man. He was perfect in the delicate task of assuming human nature, overcoming temptations, facing unmentionable humiliation and pain, and finally passing through the gates of death and then (thankfully) being resurrected.

Because of who He was Christ had a natural right to return to His rule in heaven as God, but now He also had an earned right to enter heaven as man. He had accomplished a work on earth that represented God's most remarkable ingenuity and grace.

Previously He could be called Creator; now He could also be called Savior. Previously He could rule from heaven by virtue of who He was; now He could rule because of the tests He had endured. Previously He could crush Satan with raw power; now He proved He could crush him by rescuing men from every tribe and nation out from under his evil authority. Previously He could reign as God; now He could reign as man. Above the heavens is one who was forever there, but now He is there as man as well as God.

Christ now resides in the place that He owns. Appropriately, the book of Revelation places Christ "in the midst of the throne." Hymn writer Thomas Kelly put it this way:

> *The head that once was crowned with thorns*
> *Is crowned with glory now;*
> *A royal diadem adorns*
> *The mighty Victor's brow.*
>
> *The highest place that heaven affords*
> *Is His, is His by right;*
> *The King of kings and Lord of lords*
> *And heaven's eternal light.*

Surely heaven fell silent with breathless wonder upon Christ's arrival. God the Son had arrived with the sure knowledge that a mission had been accomplished.

Psalm 24 was sung by the people of Israel in processions during a major festival. As the worshipers walked up the hill of Zion they would sing:

> *Lift up your heads, O gates,*
> *And be lifted up, O ancient doors,*
> *That the King of Glory may come in!*
> *Who is the King of glory?*
> *The LORD strong and mighty,*
> *The LORD mighty in battle.*
> *Lift up your heads, O gates,*
> *And lift them up, O, ancient doors,*
> *That the King of glory may come in!*
> *Who is this King of glory?*
> *The LORD of hosts,*
> *He is the King of glory.*

Understandably, the early church related this psalm to Jesus as He ascended into the heavenly temple. He left earth in a different condition than He found it and changed heaven after He arrived. The arrival of the King makes every head turn in adoring wonder.

The Right to Headship

Christ arrived in heaven as the head of a whole new race. The firstborn Son had begotten many sons through his work on the cross. "For whom He foreknew, He also predestined to become conformed to the image of His Son, that He might be the first-born among many brethren" (Romans 8:29). These sons whom He brought into glory (you and I) are now a part of the church, of which He is the head.

What is the purpose of this headship? Paul says that God "seated Him at His right hand in the heavenly places, far above all rule and authority and power and dominion, and every name that is named, not only in this age, but also in the one to come. And He put all things in subjection under His feet, and gave Him as head over all things to the church, which is His body, the fullness of Him who fills all in all" (Ephesians 1:20-23).

As head, Christ fulfills important responsibilities: first, He strengthens us. We share His life. We are not expected to walk through this life in our own strength. Paul wrote that Christ is the head "from whom the entire body, being supplied and held together by the joints and ligaments, grows with a growth which is from God" (Colossians 2:19). Just how are we connected to Christ? Through the gift of the Holy Spirit, which was given to God's people after the ascension: "Having been exalted to the right hand of God, and having received from the Father the promise of the Holy Spirit, He has poured forth this which you both see and hear" (Acts 2:33).

We share Christ's life, just like the head shares the same life as the rest of the body. And since the head has gone on before, the members will surely follow.

Second, He unites us with one another. By the Holy Spirit we grow together until the body is complete. Ephesians 4:15 says that "we are to grow up in all aspects into Him, who is the head, even Christ." We show our loyalty to His headship when we obey all of His commands, especially the command that we are to love one another. This is a unity that should transcend even denominational commitments.

Third, Christ represents us to the Father. He entered into the heavenly sanctuary not just as conqueror, but also to assume the role of High Priest. "Since then we have a great high priest who has passed through the heavens, Jesus the Son of God, let us hold fast our confession. For we do not have a high priest who cannot sympathize with our weaknesses, but One who has been tempted in all things as we are, yet without sin" (Hebrews 4:14,15).

Paul taught that Christ's presence at God's right hand undercut Satan's right to accuse us: "Who will bring a charge against God's elect? God is the one who justifies; who is the one who condemns? Christ Jesus is He who died, yes, rather who was raised, who is *at the right hand of God*, who also *intercedes* for us" (Romans 8:33,34, emphasis added).

Does Christ actually pray to the Father on our behalf? Perhaps. But His very presence as our representative at the right hand of God assures us that we stand fully received in the Father's presence. In the words of Charles Wesley:

> *Five bleeding wounds He bears,*
> *Received on Calvary.*
> *They pour effectual prayers;*
> *They strongly plead for me.*
> *"Forgive him, oh, forgive," they cry ....*
> *"Nor let that ransomed sinner die."*

Fourth, Christ is with us. Let's not think of Christ as so far removed that He is only remotely affected by our personal pain and struggles. The opposite is the case: He taught His disciples that it is better that He go away so that the Comforter, who would abide with us forever, would be sent. True, Christ's body can be in only one place at one time, but by His Spirit He is constantly with all of His people. He stands with us in our need, no matter where we are.

To remind yourself of the nearness of Christ, think of Him as standing next to you in the room, riding in the car with you, or walking with you as you go to work. (What T.V. programs might we not watch if Christ sat on the couch with us?)

Yes, we should think of His resurrected physical body as being in heaven, but even in body He might be nearer to us than we realize. Heaven might seem far away, but that is simply because of our concept of distance. With God, millions of miles are reduced to milliseconds, the concept of distance as a limitation vanishes. G. Campbell Morgan, thinking of the soldiers in World War II, wrote, "He can most certainly, suddenly, gloriously appear upon the field of battle to a dying soul."

Apparently Christ sometimes leaves His seat to stand at the Father's right hand. Read what happened when Stephen was about to be stoned by an angry mob: "Being full of the Holy Spirit, [Stephen] gazed intently into heaven and saw the glory of God, and Jesus standing at the right hand of God; and he said, 'Behold, I see the heavens opened up and the Son of Man standing at the right hand of God'" (Acts 7:55,56). Christ was not too busy to take note of a servant who was about to experience the pain of martyrdom. Whatever else may have been happening on the planet at that moment, Stephen had Christ's full attention. Our trials never escape His notice; the heavenly circuits are never overloaded.

When Saul was en route to Damascus to continue his persecution of believers, Christ appeared to him physically. He asked, "Saul, Saul, why are you persecuting Me?" (Acts 9:4). Christ's question not only caught Saul's attention, but also put to rest the idea that in heaven Christ just might be too preoccupied to be aware of our personal needs. When Christ's people hurt, He hurts. When they feel alienated and rejected, He feels likewise. He is "touched with the feeling of our infirmities" (Hebrews 4:15).

If we ask how Christ as man can keep track of all that is happening in the lives of millions of believers simultaneously, we must appeal to His deity. What a man cannot do, the God-man can. Remember, His Spirit pervades the whole universe. Speaking of our High Priest, the author of Hebrews writes, "There is no creature hidden from His sight, but all things are open and laid bare to the eyes of Him with whom we have to do" (Hebrews 4:13).

As the head of the church, Christ is not about to neglect His duties. His ascension is a sign of His headship.

The Right to Kingship

Christ's triumphant arrival in heaven also signifies his Kingship. He arrived as the undisputed ruler of the universe. Paul described Christ as ascending "far above all rule and authority and power and dominion, and every name that is named, not only in this world but also in the one to come" (Ephesians 1:21). In Hebrews we read that Christ "passed through the heavens" (4:14).

The point of these passages is not *distance,* but *dominion*— not *travel,* but *triumph.* Christ is not just above any other name (or any other god) in space, but He is above them in power, authority, and victory. However neglected He might be today, He stands without any serious rival whatsoever in the universe.

En route to heaven, Christ might well have been beset with the concentrated opposition of Satan and all of his hosts; while Christ was ascending "the prince of the power of the air" (Ephesians 2:2) would have launched more of his many desperate but fruitless attacks against the Son of God. Christ sustained these attacks without any hint of failing, for His victory had already been accomplished.

Think of this: Christ will never increase in strength for He is already *omnipotent*; He will never increase in His knowledge for He is already *omniscient*; He will never be given a larger kingdom for He is already *omnipresent*. He is not waiting to be crowned king; rather, He is waiting to be recognized as king. Everything and everyone is already under His feet.

Yes, He rules even now.

Look at the world, and you might never guess it was being ruled by an omnipotent king. How do we reconcile a world that is out of control morally and spiritually with the leadership of a king who has all power and authority? We must be patient with those who question Christ's performance, for it does not appear as if He is bringing order out of chaos.

Just look at the city of man with its wealth and power; just think of the abortion industry and the politically correct historians who want to cut God from our textbooks. Consider the homosexual lobby with its insidious agenda of lowering the age of consensual sex so as to justify pedophilia; just think of the political liberals intent on curbing the rights of Christians at every opportunity. If we could, we would bring judgment against them! We, like the disciples, would like to call fire down from heaven and consume them for the good of America, for the good of our families, and for the good of God!

Why does Christ not do that Himself? Why does He not intervene and clean up Washington, the liberal lobbyists, and the

Supreme Court? If Christ does not lack for power, love, and authority, why does He not bring an evil world to its senses? Atheists find that their best argument for the conclusion that there is no God is God's apparent indifference to human misery. Skeptics ask whether the King of the universe is doing His job. If He does not lack for power, does He lack the mercy that would put an end to the madness in our world? Does He care?

The problem, of course, is not just America. Wars are destroying many other countries. Women are being raped; children are being abused. In some parts of the world famine is killing thousands of people every day. In our own country, marriages are being torn apart and drugs are destroying our young people. Who can comprehend the terror, the fear, and the buckets of tears shed every hour on this hapless planet? Why would a king allow His kingdom to be overtaken by rebels?

We must distinguish two aspects to Christ's rule. Today He rules from heaven, exercising divine restraint. Indeed multiplied millions do not even acknowledge His existence, much less do they own Him as king. Daily He is insulted, either because of neglect, misrepresentation, or being classified as simply one among many. This is what happens today, but tomorrow it will be different.

Christ is waiting, "but He, having offered one sacrifice for sins for all time, sat down at the right hand of God, waiting from that time onward until His enemies be made a footstool for His feet" (Hebrews 10:12,13). Today He is waiting, biding His time until He will come to exercise His right as king in the presence of all men. His present rule from heaven is one of divine restraint.

Why does He wait? He is letting history prove a point—namely, that man cannot rule the world. He has delegated His rule to the kings and princes of this world, letting them exercise their authority as they see fit. Of course their influence is limited by the divine will and purpose so that we can confidently say that God's will is being done on earth. History is marching toward a goal.

The wait will come to an end when Christ returns to the Mount of Olives in splendor and glory. Then He will take direct control, subduing His enemies and bringing the world to justice. Then He will fulfill the ancient prophecy in Isaiah 2:4: "He will judge between the nations, and will render decisions for many peoples; and they will hammer their swords into plowshares, and their spears into pruning hooks. Nation will not lift up sword against nation, and never again will they learn war."

The present and future aspects of Christ's rule can be seen by putting the following two Bible passages together: On the one hand Paul says that God has already "put all things in subjection under His feet" (Ephesians 1:22), and on the other hand he speaks of it as a future event: "Then comes the end, when He delivers up the kingdom to the God and Father, when He has abolished all rule and all authority and power. For He must reign until He has put all His enemies under His feet" (1 Corinthians 15:24,25).

If every name that is named is already under Christ's feet, why must He wait until every enemy is finally brought under His subjection? As I explained, Christ is a king in waiting; He is a man who has been crowned in heaven but not yet acknowledged as king on earth. His coronation by God has been relatively private; the recognition of it on planet earth will be very public indeed.

Be clear about this: Christ is just as much a king when He is waiting as when He is winning! He is just as much a king in His ascent as He will be at His descent. He is just as much in control in heaven as He will be on earth. For now He is content to direct the affairs of planet earth through erring representatives; He is willing to let Satan roam the earth like a criminal who has skipped bail. For now the rebels have taken over the premises. But the day is coming when the only king whom God recognizes will be acknowledged by every tongue ever created:

> Therefore God highly exalted Him, and bestowed on Him the name which is above every name, that at the name of Jesus every knee should bow, of those who are in heaven, and on the earth, and under the earth, and that every tongue should confess that Jesus Christ is Lord, to the glory of God the Father (Philippians 2:9-11).

Our Participation in Christ's Victory

Today the drama is played out in defiance of the rightful king, but at the curtain call the rightful king will appear. The saga will end so differently from how it all began. We can be confident that every person will be called to account before God, and the books will be opened, and every individual will be judged. The record will be set straight and the facts will come out. All the false gods of this world will be exposed and the motives of men's hearts will be made plain.

For citizens of the city of God, Christ's ascension means that we have been joined with Christ in His victory. Ephesians 2:6 says that God has "raised us up with Him, and seated us with Him in the heavenly places, in Christ Jesus." You and I as believers are already in heaven, heirs to an incredible inheritance. Christ promised that He would prepare a place for us. There is a crown that only you can wear, a mansion that only you can enter. Peter said there is a place "reserved in heaven for you" (1 Peter 1:4). The only way we can be cast out of heaven is if Christ Himself is thrown out! He represents us, protecting our interests.

What Christ has by divine right was purchased for us by divine mercy. We will never become what He is, but we shall enjoy what He has. We can only stand amazed at the greatness of God's grace: "There shall no longer be any night; and they shall not have need of the light of a lamp nor the light of the sun, because the Lord God shall illumine them; and they shall reign forever and ever" (Revelation 22:5).

Christianity is often faulted because of its teaching on the depravity of mankind—the fact that we cannot do a single work that will merit the approval of God. Although no other religion insists on a person's utter sinfulness, there is none other that lifts a person to greater heights of saintliness. Christ takes us from the mud and invites us to walk on marble; He takes us from the pit and invites us to live in the palace. No other religion brings us so low and exalts us so high.

Earlier in this book I mentioned that Savonarola gained fame as a preacher in Florence. He tried to clean up the city's morals and predicted a flood of judgment would come upon the city if it did not repent. He attacked the lax, corrupt citizens through fiery preaching and censorship. During a carnival in 1496 he orchestrated "the bonfire of the vanities"—a ceremony in which people brought their gambling artifacts, lewd books, and cosmetics to be burned.

Savonarola was excommunicated for refusing to stop preaching against the Pope, and later was tried for heresy and executed. Despite the reversals he experienced, and though the truth did not triumph in his day, before his death he said, "He who believes that Christ rules above need not fear what happens below!"

C.S. Lewis was right when he said that the Christians who did the most for the present world were those who thought most of the next. "It is since Christians have largely ceased to think of the other world that they have become so ineffective in this one. Aim at heaven and you will get earth 'thrown in.' Aim at earth and you will get neither."

Others have walked before us in the fight for truth, justice, and the proclamation of the gospel. Malcolm Muggeridge said, "All news is old news happening to new people." There is nothing happening in the world that is news to God; it is all old news known from before the foundation of the world. Christ reigns in heaven today, fully in charge of our fallen world. And although we do not yet see all things under His feet, that day is coming closer. Those who believe that He reigns from heaven need not fear what happens on earth.

Take heart!

Peter Marshall was right: "It is better to fail in that which will ultimately succeed than to succeed in that which shall eventually fail." It is better to fail while fighting for the city of God than to succeed promoting the city of man. It is better to save one's soul than to gain the whole world.

We do not have to triumph in this life in order to triumph in the next. We simply need to be faithful in doing what God has asked of us. The one thing that is certain is the final victory of our Leader and our God.

Good-bye to the city of man; welcome to the eternal city of God.

The kingdom of the world has become the kingdom of our Lord, and of His Christ; and He will reign forever and ever.
—Revelation 11:15

Notes

Introduction: What Kind of Cross Does the World See?

1. Some of the material in this introduction is adapted from my book *Hitler's Cross*. The quotation from Heine is from Robert G. Waite, *Adolf Hitler, the Psychopathic God* (New York: Basic Books, 1977), p. 261.
2. Quoted in John Stott, *The Cross of Christ* (Downer's Grove, IL: InterVarsity, 1986), p. 44.

Chapter 1—The Cross and Culture Clash

1. St. Augustine, *The City of God* (New York: Image Books, 1953), bk. 15, chapter 1.
2. Ibid., bk. 14, chapter 4.

Chapter 2—The Cross and the Flag

1. Edward Dobson, "Taking Politics Out of the Sanctuary" *Liberty*, January/February 1997, p. 11.
2. As quoted in *World* magazine (August 18, 1998), p. 20.
3. Cal Thomas, "Christian Coalition Has Strayed Too Far from Its True Calling," Los Angeles Times Syndicate, 1997.
4. Edward Dobson, "Taking Politics Out of the Sanctuary," p. 11.

Chapter 3—What God Thinks of the Cross

1. Randall Terry, *Why Does a Nice Guy Like Me Keep Getting Thrown in Jail?* (Lafayette, LA: Huntington House, 1993), pp. 63-64.
2. Quoted in *Spirit Empowered Preaching* by Arturo G. Azurdia (Great Britain: Christian Focus Publications), p. 14.
3. Quoted by Tom Sine in *Cease Fire* (Grand Rapids: Eerdmans, 1995), p. 66.

4. Quoted in John Armstrong, *When God Moves* (Eugene, OR: Harvest House, 1998), pp. 65-66.

5. Quoted in Erwin Lutzer, *Hitler's Cross* (Chicago: Moody Press, 1995), pp. 152-53.

Chapter 4—What Man Thinks of the Cross

1. Tom Sine, *Cease Fire* (Grand Rapids: Eerdman's, 1995), p. 259.

Chapter 5—The Cross, the Suffering of God

1. Quoted in Charles Ohlrich, *The Suffering of God* (Downer's Grove: InterVarsity Press, 1982), p. 20.

2. Quoted in John Stott, *The Cross of Christ* (Downer's Grove: InterVarsity Press, 1986), p. 134.

3. Ibid., p. 141.

4. Ibid., p. 160.

5. Ibid., p. 151.

6. Dennis Ngien, "The God Who Suffers," *Christianity Today,* Feb. 3, 1997, p. 40.

7. Stott, *The Cross of Christ,* p. 153.

8. Ibid., p. 153.

9. Ibid., p. 156.

10. Ibid., p. 158.

11. Ngien, "The God Who Suffers," p. 41.

12. Cited in Eberhard Bethge, *Bonhoeffer: Exile and Martyr* (New York: Seabury, 1975), p. 155.

13. *The Suffering of God,* p. 108.

Chapter 6—The Cross of Reconciliation

1. Spencer Perkins, "Playing the Grace Card," *Christianity Today,* July 13, 1998, pp. 42-43.

2. Quoted by Perkins, "Playing the Grace Card," p. 43.

3. Tom Sine, *Cease Fire* (Grand Rapids: Eerdmans, 1995), p. 261.

Chapter 7—The Cross, the Basis of Moral Sanity

1. Michael S. Horton, *Beyond Culture Wars* (Chicago: Moody Press, 1994), p. 38.

2. David F. Wells, "Our Dying Culture" in *Here We Stand,* James Montgomery Boice, ed. (Grand Rapids: Baker Books, 1996), p. 30.

3. Horton, *Beyond Culture Wars,* p. 216.

4. Ibid., p. 239.

5. Jim Cymbala, *Fresh Wind, Fresh Fire* (Grand Rapids: Zondervan, 1997), p. 19.

6. Ibid., p. 57.

Chapter 8—The Cross: Standing Out in the World

1. Ed Dobson, "Taking Politics out of the Sanctuary," *Liberty,* January/February 1997.

Chapter 9—The Triumph of the Crucified

1. *World* magazine (August 18, 1998), p. 20.

2. Some of the material in this chapter was adapted from my book *Christ Among Other Gods* (Chicago: Moody Press, 1994).

Other Good
Harvest House Reading

When God Moves
John Armstrong

Many Christians today are genuinely seeking revival. Many claim to be experiencing true revival as God "awakens" them, insisting that certain happenings in today's church are truly the work of the Holy Spirit. Other believers are wary, pointing out excesses and seeming contradictions with Scripture. John Armstrong, editor of Reformation & Revival Journal, clarifies what genuine revival is, both biblically and historically.

The Heart of Christianity
Ron Rhodes

This book, excellent for believers and seekers alike, explores how the major doctrines of Christianity, including God, man, salvation, the church, angels, and the afterlife, relate directly to Christ.

Ready with an Answer
John Ankerberg and John Weldon

Answers to the top ten questions skeptics ask with powerful evidence for the truth of Christianity. From creation to salvation to the second coming of Jesus, this book explores the uniqueness of Christianity.